CAMBRIDGE LIBRARY COLLECTION

Books of enduring scholarly value

History

The books reissued in this series include accounts of historical events and movements by eye-witnesses and contemporaries, as well as landmark studies that assembled significant source materials or developed new historiographical methods. The series includes work in social, political and military history on a wide range of periods and regions, giving modern scholars ready access to influential publications of the past.

A First Year in Canterbury Settlement

Samuel Butler (1835–1902) became famous with his satirical Utopian novel *Erewhon*, based on his experiences as a sheep farmer in New Zealand and published, initially anonymously, in 1872. This earlier book, published in London in 1863 while he was still abroad, is a compilation of his letters home. Having obtained a degree in Classics from Cambridge, Butler had left England in 1859 with generous funding from his father, who hoped that making his fortune in the colonies would cure his son's ambition to become an artist. Butler was highly successful in his farming enterprise, and his letters provide both financial details and information on the practicalities of animal husbandry, pasture management and colonial life. Butler also explored Canterbury and travelled to the Southern Alps, and describes vividly the landscapes, flora and fauna of South Island. This classic source for New Zealand history also sheds light on Butler's later work.

Cambridge University Press has long been a pioneer in the reissuing of out-of-print titles from its own backlist, producing digital reprints of books that are still sought after by scholars and students but could not be reprinted economically using traditional technology. The Cambridge Library Collection extends this activity to a wider range of books which are still of importance to researchers and professionals, either for the source material they contain, or as landmarks in the history of their academic discipline.

Drawing from the world-renowned collections in the Cambridge University Library, and guided by the advice of experts in each subject area, Cambridge University Press is using state-of-the-art scanning machines in its own Printing House to capture the content of each book selected for inclusion. The files are processed to give a consistently clear, crisp image, and the books finished to the high quality standard for which the Press is recognised around the world. The latest print-on-demand technology ensures that the books will remain available indefinitely, and that orders for single or multiple copies can quickly be supplied.

The Cambridge Library Collection will bring back to life books of enduring scholarly value (including out-of-copyright works originally issued by other publishers) across a wide range of disciplines in the humanities and social sciences and in science and technology.

A First Year in
Canterbury Settlement

Samuel Butler

CAMBRIDGE
UNIVERSITY PRESS

CAMBRIDGE UNIVERSITY PRESS

Cambridge, New York, Melbourne, Madrid, Cape Town,
Singapore, São Paolo, Delhi, Tokyo, Mexico City

Published in the United States of America by Cambridge University Press, New York

www.cambridge.org
Information on this title: www.cambridge.org/9781108039383

This edition first published 1863
This digitally printed version 2011

ISBN 978-1-108-03938-3 Paperback

CANTERBURY SETTLEMENT.

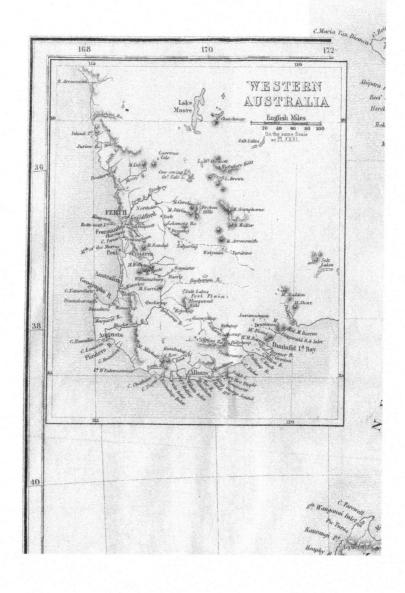

WESTERN
AUSTRALIA

English Miles

20 40 60 80 100

On the same Scale
as Pl.XXXI.

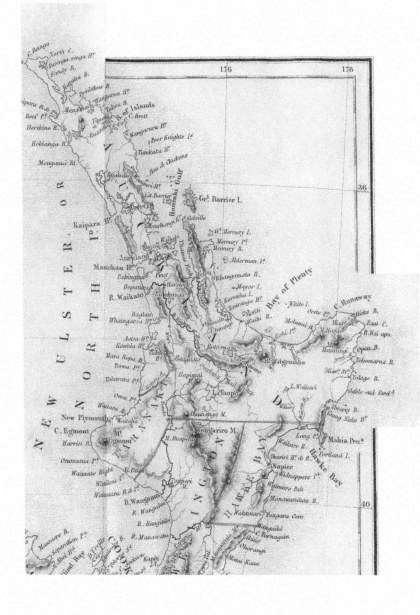

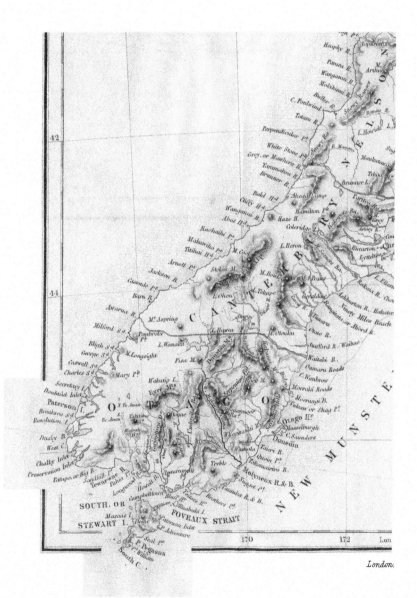

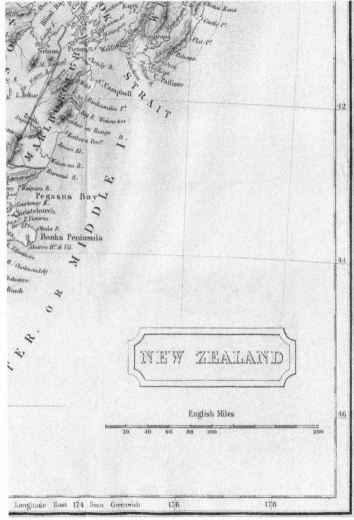

42

44

NEW ZEALAND

English Miles

20   40   60   80   100   200

46

Longman & Co.   Edwd. Weller.

A FIRST YEAR

IN

CANTERBURY SETTLEMENT.

BY

SAMUEL BUTLER.

LONDON:

LONGMAN, GREEN, LONGMAN, ROBERTS, & GREEN.

1863.

PREFACE.

———+———

THE writer of the following pages, having resolved on emigrating to New Zealand, took his passage in the ill-fated ship 'Burmah,' which never reached her destination, and is believed to have perished with all on board. His berth was chosen, and the passage-money paid, when important alterations were made in the arrangements of the vessel, in order to make room for some stock which was being sent out to the Canterbury Settlement.

The space left for the accommodation of the passengers being thus curtailed, and the comforts of the voyage seeming likely to be much diminished, the writer was most providentially induced to change his ship, and, a few weeks later, secured a berth in another vessel.

The Work is compiled from the actual letters and

journal of a young emigrant, with extracts from two papers contributed by him to the ' Eagle,' a periodical issued by some of the members of St. John's College, Cambridge, at which the writer took his degree. This variety in the sources from which the materials are put together must be the apology for some defects in their connection and coherence. It is hoped also that the circumstances of bodily fatigue and actual difficulty under which they were often written, will excuse many faults of style.

For whatever of presumption may appear in giving this little book to the public, the friends of the writer alone are answerable. It was at their wish only that he consented to its being printed. It is, however, submitted to the reader, in the hope that the unbiassed impressions of colonial life, as they fell freshly on a young mind, may not be wholly devoid of interest. Its value to his friends at home is not diminished by the fact, that the MS., having been sent out to New Zealand for revision, was, on its return, lost in the ' Colombo,' and was fished up from the Indian Ocean so nearly washed out, as to have been with some difficulty deciphered.

It should be further stated, for the encouragement

of those who think of following the example of the author, and emigrating to the same settlement, that his most recent letters indicate that he has no reason to regret the step that he has taken, and that the results of his undertaking have hitherto fully justified his expectations.

LANGAR RECTORY:
June 29, 1863.

CONTENTS.

———+———

CHAPTER I.

CHAPTER II.

CHAPTER III.

CHAPTER IV.

A FIRST YEAR

IN

CANTERBURY SETTLEMENT.

———+———

CHAPTER I.

Embarkation at Gravesend — Arrest of Passenger — Tilbury
Fort — Deal — Bay of Biscay Gale — Becalmed off Teneriffe
— Fire in the Galley — Trade Winds — Belt of Calms — Death
on Board — Shark — Current — SE. Trade Winds — Temperature — Birds — Southern Cross — Cyclone.

IT is a windy, rainy day—cold withal; a little boat is
putting off from the pier at Gravesend, and making for
a ship that is lying moored in the middle of the river;
therein are some half-dozen passengers and a lot of
heterogeneous-looking luggage; among the passengers,
and the owner of some of the most heterogeneous of
the heterogeneous luggage, is myself. The ship is an
emigrant ship, and I am one of the emigrants.

On having clambered over the ship's side and found
myself on deck, I was somewhat taken aback with the
apparently inextricable confusion of everything on

B

board; the slush upon the decks, the crying, the kiss-
ing, the mustering of the passengers, the stowing away
of baggage still left upon the decks, the rain and the
gloomy sky created a kind of half-amusing, half-dis-
tressing bewilderment, which I could plainly see to be
participated in by most of the other landsmen on board.
Honest country agriculturists and their wives were
looking as though they wondered what it would end in;
some were sitting on their boxes and making a show
of reading tracts which were being presented to them
by a serious-looking gentleman in a white tie; but all
day long they had perused the first page only, at least
I saw none turn over the second.

And so the afternoon wore on, wet, cold, and comfortless—no dinner served on account of the general
confusion. The emigration commissioner was taking a
final survey of the ship and shaking hands with this,
that, and the other of the passengers. Fresh arrivals
kept continually creating a little additional excitement
—these were saloon passengers, who alone were per-
mitted to join the ship at Gravesend. By and by a
couple of policemen made their appearance and arrested
one of the party, a London cabman, for debt. He had
a large family, and a subscription was soon started to
pay the sum he owed. Subsequently, a much larger
subscription would have been made in order to have
him taken away by anybody or anything.

Little by little the confusion subsided. The emigration commissioner left; at six we were at last allowed some victuals. Unpacking my books and arranging them in my cabin filled up the remainder of the evening, save the time devoted to a couple of meditative pipes. The emigrants went to bed, and when, at about ten o'clock, I went up for a little time upon the poop, I heard no sound save the clanging of the clocks from the various churches of Gravesend, the pattering of rain upon the decks, and the rushing of the river as it gurgled against the ship's side.

Early next morning the cocks began to crow vociferously. We had about sixty couple of the oldest inhabitants of the hen-roost on board, which were intended for the consumption of the saloon passengers —a destiny which they have since fulfilled: young fowls die on shipboard, only old ones standing the weather about the line. Besides this, the pigs began grunting and the sheep gave vent to an occasional feeble bleat, the only expression of surprise or discontent which I heard them utter during the remainder of their existence, for now, alas! they are no more. I remember dreaming I was in a farm-yard, and woke as soon as it was light. Rising immediately, I went on deck and found the morning calm and sulky—no rain, but everything very wet and very grey. There was Tilbury Fort, so different from Stanfield's dashing picture. There was Gravesend, which but a year before I had passed on my way to Antwerp with so little notion that I should ever leave it thus. Musing in this way, and taking a last look at the green fields of old England, soaking with rain, and comfortless though they then looked, I soon became aware that we had weighed anchor, and that a small steam-tug which had been getting her steam up for some little time had already begun to subtract a mite of the distance between ourselves and New Zealand. And so, early in the morning of Saturday, October 1, 1859, we started on our voyage.

The river widened out hour by hour. Soon our little steam-tug left us. A fair wind sprung up, and at two o'clock, or thereabouts, we found ourselves off Ramsgate. Here we anchored and waited till the tide, early next morning. This took us to Deal, off which we again remained a whole day. On Monday morning we weighed anchor, and since then we have had it on the forecastle, and trust we may have no further occasion for it until we arrive at New Zealand.

I will not waste time and space by describing the horrible sea-sickness of most of the passengers, a misery which I did not myself experience, nor yet will I prolong the narrative of our voyage down the channel—it was short and eventless. The captain says there is more danger between Gravesend and the Start Point (where we lost sight of land) than all the way between there and New Zealand. Fogs are so frequent and collisions occur so often. Our own passage was free from adventure. In the Bay of Biscay the water assumed a blue hue of almost incredible depth; there, moreover, we had our first touch of a gale—not that it deserved to be called a gale in comparison with what we have since experienced, still we learnt what double-reefs meant. After this the wind fell very light, and continued so for a few days. On referring to my diary, I perceive that on the 10th of October we had only got as far south as the forty-first parallel of latitude, and late on that night a heavy squall coming up from the SW. brought a foul wind with it. It soon freshened, and by two o'clock in the morning the noise of the flapping sails, as the men were reefing them, and of the wind roaring through the rigging, was deafening. All next day we lay hove to under a close-reefed main-topsail, which, being interpreted, means that the only sail set was the main-topsail, and that that was close reefed; moreover, that the ship was laid at right angles to the wind and the yards braced sharp up. Thus a ship drifts very slowly, and remains steadier than she would otherwise; she ships few or no seas, and, though she rolls a good deal, is much more easy and safe than when running at all near the wind. Next day we drifted due north, and on the third day, the fury of the gale having somewhat moderated, we resumed—not our course, but a course only four points off it. The next several days we were baffled by foul winds, jammed down on the coast of Portugal; and then we had another gale from the south, not such a one as the last, but still enough to drive us many miles out of our course; and then it fell calm, which was almost worse, for when the wind fell the sea rose, and we were tossed about in such a manner as would have forbidden even Morpheus himself to sleep. And so we crawled on till, on the morning of the 24th of October, by which time, if we had had anything like luck, we should have been close on the line, we found ourselves about thirty miles from the Peak of Teneriffe, becalmed. This was a long way out of our course, which lay three or four degrees to the westward at the very least; but the sight of the Peak was a great treat, almost compensating for past misfortunes. The Island of Teneriffe lies in latitude 28°, longitude 16°. It is about sixty miles long; towards the southern extremity the Peak towers upwards to a height of 12,300 feet, far above the other land of the island, though that too is very elevated and rugged. Our telescopes revealed serrated gullies upon the mountain sides, and showed us the fastnesses of the island in a manner that made us long to explore them. We deceived ourselves with the hope that some speculative fisherman might come out to us with oranges and grapes for sale. He would have realised a handsome sum if he had, but unfortunately none was aware of the advantages offered, and so we looked and longed in vain. The other islands were Palma, Gomera, and Ferro, all of them lofty, especially Palma—all of them beautiful. On the seaboard of Palma we could detect houses innumerable; it seemed to be very thickly inhabited and carefully cultivated. The calm continuing three days, we took stock of the islands pretty minutely, clear as they were, and rarely obscured even by a passing cloud; the weather was blazing hot, but beneath the awning it was very delicious; a calm, however, is a monotonous thing even when an island like Teneriffe is in view, and we soon tired both of it and of the gambols of the blackfish (a species of whale), and the operations on board an American vessel hard by.

On the evening of the third day a light air sprung up, and we watched the islands gradually retire into the distance. Next morning they were faint and shrunken, and by mid-day they were gone. The wind was the commencement of the north-east trades. On the next day (Thursday, October 27, lat. 27° 40′) the cook was boiling some fat in a large saucepan, when the bottom burnt through and the fat fell out over the fire, got lighted, and then ran about the whole galley, blazing and flaming as though it would set the place on fire, whereat an alarm of fire was raised, the effect of which was electrical: there was no real danger about the affair, for a fire is easily extinguishable on a ship when only above board; it is when it breaks out in the hold, is unperceived, gains strength, and finally bursts its prison, that it becomes a serious matter to extinguish it. This was quenched in five minutes, but the faces of the female steerage passengers were awful. I noticed about many a peculiar contraction and elevation of one eyebrow, which I had never seen before on the living human face, though often in pictures. I do n't mean to say that all the faces of all the saloon passengers were void of any emotion whatever.

The trades carried us down to latitude 9°. They were but light while they lasted, and left us soon. There is no wind more agreeable than the NE. trades. The sun keeps the air deliciously warm, the breeze deliciously fresh. The vessel sits bolt upright, steering a SSW. course, with the wind nearly aft: she glides along with scarcely any perceptible motion; sometimes, in the cabin, one would fancy one must be on dry land. The sky is of a greyish blue, and the sea silver grey, with a very slight haze round the horizon. The water is very smooth, even with a wind which would elsewhere raise a considerable sea. In lat. 19°, long. 25°, we first fell in with flying fish. These are usually in flocks, and are seen in greatest abundance in the morning; they fly a great way and very well, not with the kind of jump which a fish takes when springing out of the water, but with a bonâ fide flight, sometimes close to the water, sometimes some feet above it. One flew on board, and measured roughly eighteen inches between the tips of its wings. On Saturday, November 5, the trades left us suddenly after a thunder-storm, which gave us an opportunity of seeing chain lightning, which

I only remember to have seen once in England. As soon as the storm was over, we perceived that the wind was gone, and knew that we had entered that unhappy region of calms which extends over a belt of some five degrees rather to the north of the line.

We knew that the weather about the line was often calm, but had pictured to ourselves a gorgeous sun, golden sunsets, cloudless sky, and sea of the deepest blue. On the contrary, such weather is never known there, or only by mistake. It is a gloomy region. Sombre sky and sombre sea. Large cauliflower-headed masses of dazzling cumulus tower in front of a background of lavender-coloured satin. There are clouds of every shape and size. The sails idly flap as the sea rises and falls with a heavy regular but windless swell. Creaking yards and groaning rudder seem to lament that they cannot get on. The horizon is hard and black, save when blent softly into the sky upon one quarter or another by a rapidly approaching squall. A puff of wind —'Square the yards!'—the ship steers again; another— she moves slowly onward; it blows—she slips through the water; it blows hard—she runs; very hard—she flies; a drop of rain—the wind lulls; three or four more of the size of half-a-crown—it falls very light; it rains hard, and then the wind is dead—whereon the rain comes down in a torrent which those must see who would believe. The air is so highly charged with moisture that any damp thing remains damp and any dry thing dampens: the decks are always wet. Mould springs up anywhere, even on the very boots which one is wearing; the atmosphere is like that of a vapour bath, and the dense clouds seem to ward off the light, but not the heat, of the sun. The dreary monotony of such weather affects the spirits of all, and even the health of some. One poor girl who had long been consumptive, but who apparently had rallied much during the voyage, seemed to give way suddenly as soon as we had been a day in this belt of calms, and four days after, we lowered her over the ship's side into the deep.

One day we had a little excitement in capturing a shark, whose triangular black fin had been veering about above water for some time at a little distance from the ship. I will not detail a process that has so often been described, but will content myself with saying that he did not die unavenged, inasmuch as he administered a series of cuffs and blows to anyone that was near him which would have done credit to a prize-fighter, and several of the men got severe handling or, I should rather say, 'tailing' from him. He was accompanied by two beautifully striped pilot fish — the never-failing attendants of the shark.

One day during this calm we fell in with a current, when the aspect of the sea was completely changed. It resembled a furiously rushing river, and had the sound belonging to a strong stream, only much intensified; the waves, too, tossed up their heads perpendicularly into the air; whilst the empty flour-casks drifted ahead of us and to one side. It was impossible to look at the sea without noticing its very singular appearance. Soon a wind springing up raised the waves and obliterated the more manifest features of the current, but for two or three days afterwards we could perceive it more or less. There is always at this time of year a strong westerly set here. The wind was the commencement of the SE. trades, and was welcomed by all with the greatest pleasure. In two days more we reached the line.

We crossed the line far too much to the west, in long. 31° 6', after a very long passage of nearly seven weeks, such as our captain says he never remembers to have made; fine winds, however, now began to favour us, and in another week we got out of the tropics, having had the sun vertically overhead, so as to have no shadow, on the preceding day. Strange to say, the weather was never at all oppressively hot after lat. 2° north, or thereabouts. A fine wind, or indeed a light wind, at sea removes all unpleasant heat even of the hottest and most perpendicular sun. The only time that we suffered any inconvenience at all from heat was during the belt of calms; when the sun was vertically over our heads it felt no hotter than on an ordinary summer day. Immediately, however, upon leaving the tropics the cold increased sensibly, and in lat. 27° 8' I find that I was not warm once all day. Since then we have none of us ever been warm, save

when taking exercise or in bed; when the thermometer
was up at 50° we thought it very high and called it warm.
The reason of the much greater cold of the southern
than of the northern hemisphere is that the former
contains so much less land.   I have not seen the thermometer below 42° in my cabin, but am sure that outside it has often been very much lower.   We almost all
got chilblains, and wondered much what the winter of
this hemisphere must be like if this was its summer:
I believe, however, that as soon as we get off the coast
of Australia, which I hope we may do in a couple of
days, we shall feel a very sensible rise in the thermometer at once.   Had we known what was coming, we
should have prepared better against it, but we were
most of us under the impression that it would be warm
summer weather all the way.   No doubt we felt it
more than we should otherwise, on account of our
having so lately crossed the line.

The great feature of the southern seas is the multi-
tude of birds which inhabit it.   Huge albatrosses,
molimorks (a smaller albatross), Cape hens, Cape
pigeons, parsons, boobies, whale birds, mutton birds,
and many more, wheel continually about the ship's
stern, sometimes in dozens, sometimes in scores, always
in considerable numbers.   If a person takes two pieces
of pork and ties them together, leaving perhaps a yard
of string between the two pieces, and then throws them
into the sea, one albatross will catch hold of one

end, and another of the other, each bolts his own
end and then tugs and fights with his rival till one or
other has to disgorge his prize; we have not, however,
succeeded in catching any, neither have we tried the
above experiment ourselves. Albatrosses are not white;
they are grey, or brown with a white streak down the
back, and spreading a little into the wings. The under
part of the bird is a bluish-white. They remain without
moving the wing a longer time than any bird that I
have ever seen, but some suppose that each individual
feather is vibrated rapidly, though in very small space,
without any motion being imparted to the main pinions
of the wing. I am informed that there is a strong
muscle attached to each of the large plumes in their
wings. It certainly is strange how so large a bird
should be able to travel so far and so fast without any
motion of the wing. Albatrosses are often entirely
brown, but farther south, and when old, I am told,
they become sometimes quite white. The stars of the
southern hemisphere are lauded by some: I cannot see
that they surpass or equal those of the northern. Some,
of course, are the same. The southern cross is a very
great delusion. It isn't a cross. It is a kite, a kite
upside down, an irregular kite upside down, with only
three respectable stars and one very poor and very
much out of place. Near it, however, is a truly mys-
terious and interesting object called the coal sack: it
is a black patch in the sky distinctly darker than all

the rest of the heavens. No star shines through it. The proper name for it is the black Magellan cloud.

We reached the Cape, passing about six degrees south of it, in twenty-five days after crossing the line, a very fair passage; and since the Cape we have done well until a week ago, when, after a series of very fine runs, and during as fair a breeze as one would wish to see, we were some of us astonished to see the captain giving orders to reef topsails. The royals were stowed, so were the top-gallant-sails, topsails close reefed, mainsail reefed, and just at 10.45 P.M., as I was going to bed, I heard the captain give the order to take a reef in the foresail and furl the mainsail; but before I was in bed a quarter of an hour afterwards, a blast of wind came up like a wall, and all night it blew a regular hurricane. The glass, which had dropped very fast all day, and fallen lower than the captain had ever seen it in the southern hemisphere, had given him warning what was coming, and he had prepared for it. That night we ran away before the wind to the north, next day we lay hove-to till evening, and two days afterwards the gale was repeated, but with still greater violence. The captain was all ready for it, and a ship, if she is a good sea-boat, may laugh at any winds or any waves provided she be prepared. The danger is when a ship has got all sail set and one of these bursts of wind is shot out at her; then her masts go overboard in no time. Sailors generally estimate a gale of wind by the amount

of damage it does, if they don't lose a mast or get their
bulwarks washed away, or at any rate carry away a few
sails, they don't call it a gale, but a stiff breeze; if, however, they are caught even by comparatively a very
inferior squall, and lose something, they call it a gale.
The captain assured us that the sea never assumes a
much grander or more imposing aspect than that which
it wore on this occasion. He called me to look at it
between two and three in the morning when it was at
its worst; it was certainly very grand, and made a
tremendous noise, and the wind would scarcely let one
stand, and made such a roaring in the rigging as I never
heard, but there was not that terrific appearance that I
had expected. It didn't suggest any ideas to one's mind
about the possibility of anything happening to one. It
was excessively unpleasant to be rolled hither and
thither, and I never felt the force of gravity such a
nuisance before; one's soup at dinner would face one
at an angle of 45° with the horizon, it would look as
though immoveable on a steep inclined plane, and it
required the nicest handling to keep the plane truly
horizontal. So with one's tea, which would alternately
rush forward to be drunk and fly as though one were a
Tantalus; so with all one's goods, which would be seized
with the most erratic propensities. Still we were unable
to imagine ourselves in any danger, save that one flaxen-
headed youth of two-and-twenty kept waking up his
companion for the purpose of saying to him at intervals

during the night, 'I say, N——, is n't it awful?' till finally
N—— silenced him with a boot. While on the subject
of storms I may add, that a captain, if at all a scientific
man, can tell whether he is in a cyclone (as we were)
or not, and if he is in a cyclone he can tell in what
part of it he is, and how he must steer so as to get out
of it. A cyclone is a storm that moves in a circle round
a calm of greater or less diameter; the calm moves
forward in the centre of the rotatory storm at the rate
of from one or two to thirty miles an hour. A large
cyclone 500 miles in diameter, rushing furiously round
its centre, will still advance in a right line, only very
slowly indeed. A small one 50 or 60 miles across will
progress more rapidly. One vessel sailed for five days
at the rate of 12, 13, and 14 knots an hour round one
of these cyclones before the wind all the time, yet in
the five days she had made only 187 miles in a straight
line. I tell this tale as it was told to me, but have not
studied the subjects myself. Whatever saloon passengers
may think about a gale of wind, I am sure that the poor
sailors who have to go aloft in it and reef topsails cannot
welcome it with any pleasure.

CHAPTER II.

BEFORE continuing the narrative of my voyage, I must
turn to other topics and give you some account of my
life on board. My time has passed very pleasantly: I
have read a good deal; I have nearly finished Gibbon's
'Decline and Fall of the Roman Empire,' am studying
Liebig's ' Agricultural Chemistry,' and learning the
concertina on the instrument of one of my fellow-
passengers. Besides this, I have had the getting up
and management of our choir. We practise three or
four times a week; we chant the Venite, Glorias, and Te
Deums, and sing one hymn. I have two basses, two
tenors, one alto, and lots of girls, and the singing
certainly is better than you would hear in nine country
places out of ten. I have been glad by this means to
form the acquaintance of many of the poorer passengers.
My health has been very good all the voyage: I have
not had a day's sea-sickness. The provisions are not
very first-rate, and the day after to-morrow, being

c

Christmas Day, we shall sigh for the roast beef of Old
England, as our dinner will be somewhat of the
meagrest.   Never mind!   On the whole I cannot see
reason to find any great fault.   We have a good ship,
a good captain, and victuals sufficient in quantity.
Everyone but myself abuses the owners like pick-
pockets, but I rather fancy that some of them will find
themselves worse off in New Zealand.   When I come
back, if I live to do so (and I sometimes amass a
wonderful fortune in a very short time, and come back
fabulously rich, and do all sorts of things), I think I
shall try the overland route.   Almost every evening
four of us have a very pleasant rubber, which never
gets stale.   So you will have gathered that, though very
anxious to get to our journey's end, which, with luck, we
hope to do in about three weeks' time, still the voyage
has not proved at all the unbearable thing that some of
us imagined it would have been.   One great amusement
I have forgotten to mention—that is, shuffle-board, a
game which consists in sending some round wooden
platters along the deck into squares chalked and numbered from one to ten.   This game will really keep one
quite hot in the coldest weather if played with spirit.

.   .   .   .

During the month that has elapsed since writing
the last sentence, we have had strong gales and long
tedious calms.   On one of these occasions the captain
lowered a boat, and a lot of us scrambled over the ship's

side and got in, taking it in turns to row. The first thing that surprised us was the very much warmer temperature of the sea-level than that on deck. The change was astonishing. I have suffered from a severe cold ever since my return to the ship. On deck it was cold, thermometer 46°; on the sea-level it was deliciously warm. The next thing that surprised us was the way in which the ship was pitching, though it appeared a dead calm. Up she rose and down she fell upon a great hummocky swell which came lazily up from the SW., making our horizon from the boat all uneven. On deck we had thought it a very slight swell; in the boat we perceived what a heavy, humpy, ungainly heap of waters kept rising and sinking all round us, sometimes blocking out the whole ship, save the top of the main royal, in the strangest way in the world. We pulled round the ship, thinking we had never in our lives seen anything so beautiful as she then looked in the sunny morning, when suddenly we saw a large ripple in the waters not far off. At first the captain imagined it to have been caused by a whale, and was rather alarmed, but by and by it turned out to be nothing but a shoal of fish. Then we made for a large piece of sea-weed which we had seen some way astern. It extended some ten feet deep, and was a huge, tangled, loose, floating mass; among it nestled little fishes innumerable, and as we looked down amid its intricate branches through the sun-lit azure of the water, the effect was

c 2

beautiful. This mass we attached to the boat, and
with great labour and long time succeeded in getting
it up to the ship, the little fishes following behind
the sea-weed. It was impossible to lift it on board,
so we fastened it to the ship's side and came in to
luncheon. After lunch some ropes were arranged to
hoist the ladies in a chair over the ship's side and lower
them into the boat—a process which created much
merriment. Into the boat we put half a dozen of
champagne—a sight which gave courage to one or two
to brave the descent who had not previously ventured
on such a feat. Then the ladies were pulled round the
ship, and, when about a mile ahead of her, we drank the
champagne and had a regular jollification. Returning
to show them the sea-weed, the little fishes looked so
good that some one thought of a certain net wherewith
the doctor catches ocean insects, porpytas, clios, spinulas,
&c. With this we caught in half an hour, amid much
screaming, laughter, and unspeakable excitement, no
less than 250 of them. They were about five inches
long—funny little blue fishes with wholesome-looking
scales. We ate them next day, and they were excellent. Some expected that we should have swollen or
suffered some bad effects, but no evil happened to us:
not but what these deep-sea fishes are frequently poisonous, but I believe that scaly fishes are always harmless.
We returned by half-past three, after a most enjoyable
day; but, as proof of the heat being much greater in

the boat, I may mention that one of the party lost the
skin from his face and arms, and that we were all much
sunburnt even in so short a time; yet one man who
bathed that day said he had never felt such cold water
in his life.

We are now (January 21) in great hopes of sighting
land in three or four days, and are really beginning to
feel near the end of our voyage : not that I can realise
this to myself; it seems as though I had always been on
board the ship, and was always going to be, and as if all
my past life had not been mine, but had belonged to
somebody else, or as though some one had taken mine
and left me his by mistake. I expect, however, that
when the land actually comes in sight we shall have
little difficulty in realising the fact that the voyage
has come to a close.   The weather has been much
warmer since we have been off the coast of Australia,
even though Australia is some 10° north of our present
position. I have not, however, yet seen the thermometer
higher than 56° since we passed the Cape. Now we are
due south of the south point of Van Diemen's Land, and
consequently nearer land than we have been for some
time. We are making for the Snares, two high islets
about sixty miles south of Stewart's Island, the southern-
most of the New Zealand group. We sail immediately
to the north of them, and then turn up suddenly.
The route we have to take passes between the Snares
and the Traps—two rather ominous-sounding names,

but I believe more terrible in name than in any other
particular.

January 22.—Yesterday at mid-day I was sitting
writing in my cabin, when I heard the joyful cry of
' Land !' and, rushing on deck, saw the swelling and
beautiful outline of the high land in Stewart's Island.
We had passed close by the Snares in the morning, but
the weather was too thick for us to see them, though the
birds flocked therefrom in myriads.   We then passed
between the Traps, which the captain saw distinctly, one
on each side of him, from the main topgallant yard.
Land continued in sight till sunset, but since then it
has disappeared.   To-day (Sunday) we are speeding
up the coast; the anchors are ready, and to-morrow
by early daylight we trust to drop them in the harbour
of Lyttelton.   We have reason, from certain newspapers,
to believe that the mails leave on the 23rd of the month,
in which case I shall have no time or means to add a
single syllable.

January 26.—Alas for the vanity of human specu-
lation !   After writing the last paragraph the wind fell
light, then sprung up foul, and so we were slowly driven
to the ENE.   On Monday night it blew hard, and we had
close-reefed topsails.   Tuesday morning at five it was
lovely, and the reefs were all shaken out; a light air
sprang up, and the ship, at 10 o'clock, had come up to
her course, when suddenly, without the smallest warning, a gale came down upon us from the SW. like a

wall. The men were luckily very smart in taking in
canvass, but at one time the captain thought he should
have had to cut away the mizenmast. We were reduced
literally to bare poles, and lay-to under a piece of tar-
paulin, six times doubled, and about two yards square,
fastened up in the mizen rigging. All day and night
we lay thus, drifting to leeward at three knots an hour.
In the twenty-four hours we had drifted sixty miles.
Next day the wind moderated; but at 12 we found that we
were eighty miles north of the peninsula and some 3° east
of it. So we set a little sail, and commenced forereach-
ing slowly on our course. Little and little the wind died,
and it soon fell dead calm. That evening (Wednesday),
some twenty albatrosses being congregated like a flock
of geese round the ship's stern, we succeeded in catching
some of them, the first we had caught on the voyage.
We would have let them go again, but the sailors think
them good eating, and begged them of us, at the same
time prophesying two days' foul wind for every albatross
taken. It was then dead calm, but a light wind sprang
up in the night, and on Thursday we sighted Bank's
Peninsula. Again the wind fell tantalisingly light, but
we kept drawing slowly toward land. In the beautiful
sunset sky, crimson and gold, blue, silver, and purple,
exquisite and tranquillising, lay ridge behind ridge, outline behind outline, sunlight behind shadow, shadow
behind sunlight, gully and serrated ravine. Hot puffs
of wind kept coming from the land, and there were

several fires burning. I got my arm-chair on deck, and smoked a quiet pipe with the intensest satisfaction. Little by little the night drew down, and then we rounded the headlands. Strangely did the waves sound breaking against the rocks of the harbour; strangely, too, looked the outlines of the mountains through the night. Presently we saw a light ahead from a ship: we drew slowly near, and as we passed you might have heard a pin drop. 'What ship's that?' said a strange voice.—'The Roman Emperor,' said the captain. 'Are you all well?'—'All well.' Then the captain asked, 'Has the Robert Small arrived?'—'No,' was the answer, 'nor yet the Burmah.'* You may imagine what I felt. Then a rocket was sent up, and the pilot came on board. He gave us a roaring republican speech on the subject of India, China, &c. I rather admired him, especially as he faithfully promised to send us some fresh beefsteaks and potatoes for breakfast. A north-wester sprung up as soon as we had dropt anchor: had it commenced a little sooner we should have had to put out again to sea. That night I packed a knapsack to go on shore, but the wind blew so hard that no boat could put off till one o'clock in the day, at which hour I and one or two others landed, and, proceeding to the post office, were told there were no letters for us. I afterwards found mine had gone hundreds of miles away to a namesake—a cruel disappointment.

* See Preface.

A few words concerning the precautions advisable for anyone who is about to take a long sea-voyage may perhaps be useful. First and foremost, unless provided with a companion whom he well knows and can trust, he must have a cabin to himself. There are many men with whom one can be on excellent terms when not compelled to be perpetually with them, but whom the propinquity of the same cabin would render simply intolerable. It would not even be particularly agreeable to be awakened during a hardly-captured wink of sleep by the question ' Is it not awful ? ' that, however, would be a minor inconvenience. No one, I am sure, will repent paying a few pounds more for a single cabin who has seen the inconvenience that others have suffered from having a drunken or disagreeable companion in so confined a space. It is not even like a large room. He should have books in plenty, both light and solid. A folding arm-chair is a great comfort, and a very cheap one. In the hot weather I found mine invaluable, and, in the bush, it will still come in usefully. He should have a little table and common chair: these are real luxuries, as all who have tried to write, or seen others attempt it, from a low arm-chair at a washing-stand will readily acknowledge. A small disinfecting charcoal filter is very desirable. Ship's water is often bad, and the ship's filter may be old and defective. Mine has secured me and others during the voyage pure and sweet-tasting water, when we could not drink that supplied us by the ship. A bottle or two of raspberry vinegar will be found a luxury when near the line. By the aid of these means and appliances I have succeeded in making myself exceedingly comfortable. A small chest of drawers would have been preferable to a couple of boxes for my clothes, and I should recommend another to get one. A ten-pound note will suffice for all these things. The bunk should not be too wide : one rolls so in rough weather; of course it should not be athwartships, if avoidable. No one in his right mind will go second class if he can, by any hook or crook, raise money enough to go first.

On the whole, there are many advantageous results from a sea-voyage. One's geography improves apace, and numberless incidents occur pregnant with interest to a landsman; moreover, there are sure to be many on board who have travelled far and wide, and one gains a great deal of information about all sorts of races and places. One effect is, perhaps, pernicious, but this will probably soon wear off on land. It awakens an adventurous spirit, and kindles a strong desire to visit almost every spot upon the face of the globe. The captain yarns about California and the China seas—the doctor about Valparaiso and the Andes —another raves about Hawaii and the Islands of the Pacific—while a fourth will compare nothing with Japan.

The world begins to feel very small when one finds

one can get half round it in three months; and one mentally determines to visit all these places before coming back again, not to mention a good many more.

I search my diary in vain to find some pretermitted adventure wherewith to give you a thrill, or, as good Mrs. B. calls it, 'a feel;' but I can find none. The mail is going; I will write again by the next.

CHAPTER III.

Aspect of Port Lyttelton — Ascent of Hill behind it — View
— Christ Church — Yankeeisms — Return to Port Lyttelton
and Ship — Phormium Tenax — Visit to a Farm — Moa
Bones.

JANUARY 27 1860.—Oh the heat! the clear trans-
parent atmosphere, and the dust! How shall I describe
everything—the little townlet, for I cannot call it town,
nestling beneath the bare hills that we had been looking
at so longingly all the morning — the scattered wooden
boxes of houses, with ragged roods of scrubby ground
between them—the tussocks of brown grass—the huge
wide-leafed flax, with its now seedy stem, sometimes 15
or 16 feet high, luxuriant and tropical-looking — the
healthy clear-complexioned men, shaggy-bearded, rowdy-
hatted, and independent, pictures of rude health and
strength — the stores, supplying all heterogeneous commodities — the mountains, rising right behind the
harbour to a height of over a thousand feet—the varied
outline of the harbour now smooth and sleeping. Ah
me! pleasant sight and fresh to sea-stricken eyes. The
hot air, too, was very welcome after our long chill.

We dined at the table d'hôte at the Mitre—so foreign

and yet so English—the windows open to the ground,
looking upon the lovely harbour. Hither come more of
the shaggy clear-complexioned men with the rowdy
hats; looked at them with awe and befitting respect.
Much grieved to find beer sixpence a glass. This was
indeed serious, and was one of the first intimations
which we received that we were in a land where money
flies like wild-fire.

After dinner I and another commenced the ascent of
the hill between port and Christ Church. We had
not gone far before we put our knapsacks on the back
of the pack-horse that goes over the hill every day
(poor pack-horse!). It is indeed an awful pull up that
hill; yet we were so anxious to see what was on the
other side of it that we scarcely noticed the fatigue :
I thought it very beautiful. It is volcanic, brown, and
dry; large intervals of crumbling soil, and then a stiff,
wiry, uncompromising-looking tussock of the very hardest grass; then perhaps a flax bush, or, as we should
have said, a flax plant; then more crumbly brown dry
soil, mixed with fine but dried grass, and then more
tussocks; volcanic rock everywhere cropping out, sometimes red and tolerably soft, sometimes black and
abominably hard. There was a great deal, too, of a very
uncomfortable prickly shrub, which they call Irishman,
and which I do not like the look of at all. There were
cattle browsing where they could, but to my eyes it
seemed as though they had but poor times of it. So

we continued to climb, panting and broiling in the afternoon sun, and much admiring the lovely view beneath.
At last we near the top, and look down upon the plain,
bounded by the distant Apennines, that run through the
middle of the island. Near at hand, at the foot of the
hill, we saw a few pretty little box-like houses in trim
pretty little gardens, stacks of corn and fields, a little
river with a craft or two lying near a wharf, whilst the
nearer country was squared into many-coloured fields.
But after all the view was rather of the 'long stare'
description. There was a great extent of country, but
very few objects to attract the eye and make it rest any
while in any given direction. The mountains wanted
outlines; they were not broken up into fine forms like
the Carnarvonshire mountains, but were rather a long,
blue, lofty, even line, like the Jura from Geneva or the
Berwyn from Shrewsbury. The plains, too, were lovely in
colouring, but would have been wonderfully improved
by an object or two a little nearer than the mountains.
I must confess that the view, though undoubtedly fine,
rather disappointed me. The one in the direction of
the harbour was infinitely superior.

At the bottom of the hill we met the car to Christ
Church; it halted some time at a little wooden public-
house, and by and by at another, where was a Methodist
preacher, who had just been reaping corn for two
pounds an acre. He showed me some half-dozen stalks
of gigantic size, but most of that along the road-

side was thin and poor. Then we reached Christ Church on the little river Avon; it is larger than Lyttelton and more scattered, but not so pretty. Here, too, the men are shaggy, clear-complexioned, brown, and healthy-looking, and wear exceedingly rowdy hats. I put up at Mr. Rowland Davis's; and as no one during the evening seemed much inclined to talk to me, I listened to the conversation.

The all-engrossing topics seemed to be sheep, horses, dogs, cattle, English grasses, paddocks, bush, and so forth. From about seven o'clock in the evening till about twelve at night I cannot say that I heard much else. These were the exact things I wanted to hear about, and I listened till they had been repeated so many times over that I almost grew tired of the subject, and wished the conversation would turn to something else. A few expressions were not familiar to me. When we should say in England ' Certainly not,' it is here ' No fear,' or ' Do n't *you* believe it.' When they want to answer in the affirmative they say ' It is *so*,' ' It does *so*.' The word ' hum,' too, without pronouncing the *u*, is in amusing requisition. I perceived that this stood either for assent, or doubt, or wonder, or a general expression of comprehension without compromising the hummer's own opinion, and indeed for a great many more things than these; in fact, if a man did not want to say anything at all he said 'hum hum.' It is a very good expression, and saves much trouble when its familiar use has been acquired. Beyond these trifles I noticed no Yankeeism, and the conversation was English in point of expression. I was rather startled at hearing one gentleman ask another whether he meant to wash this year, and receive the answer 'No.' I soon discovered that a person's sheep are himself. If his sheep are clean, he is clean. He does not wash his *sheep* before shearing, but *he* washes; and, most marvellous of all, it is not his sheep which lamb, but he 'lambs down' himself.

. . . .

I have purchased a horse, by name Doctor. I hope he is a homœopathist. He is in colour bay, distinctly branded P. C. on the near shoulder. I am glad the brand is clear, for, as you well know, all horses are alike to me unless there is some violent distinction in their colour. This horse I bought from ———, to whom Mr. Fitzgerald kindly gave me a letter of introduction. I thought I could not do better than buy from a person of known character, seeing that my own ignorance is so very great upon the subject. I had to give 55*l.*, but, as horses are going, that does not seem much out of the way. He is a good river-horse, and very strong. A horse is an absolute necessity in this settlement; he is your carriage, your coach, and your railway train.

On Friday I went to Port Lyttelton, meeting on the way many of our late fellow-passengers — some despondent, some hopeful; one or two dinnerless and in the dumps when we first encountered them, but dinnered and hopeful when we met them again on our return. We chatted with and encouraged them all, pointing out the general healthy well-conditioned look of the residents. Went on board. How strangely changed the ship appeared! Sunny, motionless, and quiet; no noisy children, no slatternly slipshod women rolling about the decks, no slush, no washing of dirty linen in dirtier water. There was the old mate in a clean shirt at last, leaning against the mainmast, and smoking his yard of clay; the butcher close-shaven and clean; the sailors smart, and welcoming us with a smile. It almost looked like going home. Dined in Lyttelton with several of my fellow-passengers, who evidently thought it best to be off with the old love before they were on with the new, i. e. to spend all they brought with them before they set about acquiring a new fortune. Then went and helped Mr. and Mrs. R. to arrange their new house, i. e. R. and I scrubbed the floors of the two rooms they have taken with soap, scrubbing-brushes, flannel, and water, made them respectably clean, and removed his boxes into their proper places.

Saturday.—Rode again to port, and saw my case of saddlery still on board. When riding back the haze obscured the snowy range, and the scenery reminded me much of Cambridgeshire. The distinctive marks which characterise it as not English are the occasional Ti palms, which have a very tropical appearance, and the luxuriance of the Phormium tenax. If you strip a shred of this leaf not thicker than an ordinary piece of string, you will find it hard work to break it, if you succeed in doing so at all without cutting your finger. On the whole, if the road leading from Heathcote Ferry to Christ Church were through an avenue of mulberry trees, and the fields on either side were cultivated with Indian corn and vineyards, and if through these you could catch an occasional glimpse of a distant cathedral of pure white marble, you might well imagine yourself nearing Milan. As it is, the country is a sort of a cross between the plains of Lombardy and the fens of North Cambridgeshire.

At night, a lot of Nelson and Wellington men came to the club. I was amused at dinner by a certain sailor and others, who maintained that the end of the world was likely to arrive shortly; the principal argument appearing to be, that there was no more sheep country to be found in Canterbury. This fact is, I fear, only too true. With this single exception, the conversation was purely horsey and sheepy. The fact is, the races are approaching, and they are the grand annual jubilee of Canterbury.

Next morning, I rode some miles into the country, and visited a farm. Found the inmates (two brothers) at dinner. Cold boiled mutton and bread, and cold tea without milk, poured straight from a huge kettle in which it is made every morning, seem the staple commodities. No potatoes—nothing hot. They had no servant, and no cow. The bread, which was very white, was made by the younger. They showed me, with some little pleasure, some of the improvements they were making, and told me what they meant to do; and I looked at them with great respect. These men were as good gentlemen, in the conventional sense of the word, as any with whom we associate in England—I daresay, *de facto*, much better than many of them. They showed me some moa bones which they had ploughed up (the moa, as you doubtless know, was an enormous bird, which must have stood some fifteen feet high), also some stone Mäori battle-axes. They bought this land two years ago, and assured me that, even though they had not touched it, they could get for it cent. per cent. upon the price which they then gave.

CHAPTER IV.

Sheep on Terms, Schedule and Explanation — Investments in
Sheep-run — Risk of Disease, and Laws upon the Subject —
Investment in laying down Land in English Grass—In Farming
— Journey to Oxford — Journey to the Glaciers — Remote
Settlers — Literature in the Bush — Blankets and Flies —
Ascent of the Rakaia — Camping out — Glaciers — Minerals
— Parrots — Unexplored Col — Burning the Flats —Return.

FEBRUARY 10, 1860.—I must confess to being fairly
puzzled to know what to do with the money you have
sent me.   Everyone suggests different investments.
One says buy sheep and put them out on terms.   I will
explain to you what this means.   I can buy a thousand
ewes for 1,250*l.*, these I should place in the charge of a
squatter whose run is not fully stocked (and indeed
there is hardly a run in the province fully stocked).
This person would take my sheep for either three, four,
five, or more years, as we might arrange, and would
allow me yearly 2*s.* 6*d.* per head in lieu of wool.
This would give me 2*s.* 6*d.* as the yearly interest
on 25*s.*   Besides this he would allow me 40 per cent.
per annum of increase, half male, and half female, and

of these the females would bear increase also as soon
as they had attained the age of two years; moreover
the increase would return me 2s. 6d. per head wool
money as soon as they became sheep. At the end of
the term, my sheep would be returned to me as per
agreement, with no deduction for deaths, but the
original sheep would be, of course, so much the older,
and some of them being doubtless dead, sheep of the same
age as they would have been will be returned in their
place.

I will subjoin a schedule showing what 500 ewes
will amount to in seven years; we will date from
January 1860, and will suppose the yearly incease to
be one-half male and one-half female.

		Ewes	Ewe Lambs	Wether Lambs	Ewe Hoggets	Wether Hoggets	Wethers	Total
January	1860	500	—	—	—	—	—	500
„	1861	500	100	100	—	—	—	700
„	1862	500	100	100	100	100	—	900
„	1863	600	120	120	100	100	100	1,140
„	1864	700	140	140	120	120	200	1,420
„	1865	820	164	164	140	140	320	1,748
„	1866	960	192	192	164	164	460	2,132
„	1867	1124	225	225	192	192	624	2,582

The yearly wool money would be :—

		£	s.	d.
January 1861	. . . .	62	10	0
„ 1862	. . . .	87	10	0
„ 1863	. . . .	112	10	0
„ 1864	. . . .	142	10	0
„ 1865	. . . .	177	10	0
„ 1866	. . . .	218	10	0
„ 1867	. . . .	266	10	0
Total wool money received	. . .	£1,067	10	0
Original capital expended	. . . . .	£625	0	0

I will explain briefly the meaning of this.

We will suppose that the ewes have all two teeth to start with—two teeth indicate one year old, four teeth two years, six teeth three years, eight teeth (or full mouthed) four years. For the edification of some of my readers as ignorant as I am myself upon ovine matters, I may mention that the above teeth are to be looked for in the lower jaw and not the upper, the front portion of which is toothless. The ewes, then, being one year old to start with, they will be eight years old at the end of seven years. I have only however given you so long a term that you may see what would be the result of putting out sheep on terms either for three, four, five, six, or seven years, according as you like. Sheep at eight years old will be in their old age : they will live nine or ten years—sometimes more, but an eight year old sheep would be what is called a broken-mouthed

creature, that is to say it would have lost some of its
teeth from old age, and would generally be found to
crawl along at the tail end of the mob; so that of the
2,582 sheep returned to me, 500 would be very old, 200
would be seven years old, 200 six years old. All these
would pass as old sheep, and not fetch very much; one
might get about 15s. a head for the lot all round.
Perhaps, however, you might sell the 200 six years old
with the younger ones. Not to over estimate, count
these 700 old sheep as worth nothing at all, and consider that I have 1,800 sheep in prime order, reckoning
the lambs as sheep (a weaned lamb being worth nearly
as much as a full-grown sheep). Suppose these sheep
to have gone down in value from 25s. a head to 10s.,
and at the end of my term I realise 900l. Suppose
that of the wool money I have only spent 62l. 10s. per
annum, i.e. ten per cent. on the original outlay, and
that I have laid by the remainder of the wool money.
I shall have from the wool money a surplus of
630l. (some of which should have been making ten per
cent. interest for some time), that is to say my total
receipts for the sheep should be at the least 1,530l. Say
that the capital had only doubled itself in the seven
years, the investment could not be considered a bad
one. The above is a bonâ fide statement of one of the
commonest methods of investing money in sheep. I
cannot think from all I have heard that sheep will be

lower than 10s. a head, still some place the minimum value as low as 6s.*

The question arises, What is to be done with one's money when the term is out? I cannot answer; yet surely the colony cannot be quite used up in seven

---

* *Aug.* 1862.—Since writing the above, matters have somewhat changed. Firstly, Ewes are fully worth 30s. a head, and are not to be had under. Secondly, The diggings in Otago have caused the value of wethers to rise, and as they are now selling at 33s. on the runs of the Otago station (I quote the *Lyttelton Times*, which may be depended upon), and those runs are only very partially stocked, the supply there must in all probability fall short of the demand. The price of sheep in this settlement is therefore raised also, and likely to continue high. All depends upon what this next spring may bring forth upon the Otago gold fields. If they keep up the reputation which they sustained until the winter caused the diggers to retreat, the price will be high for some few years longer; if they turn out a failure, it *must* fall before very long. Still there is a large and increasing population in Canterbury, and as its sheep-feeding area is as nothing compared with that of Australia, we do not expect sheep here ever to fall as low as they did there before the diggings. Indeed, they hardly can do so; for our sheep are larger than the Australian, and clip a much heavier fleece, so that their fleece, and skins, and tallow must be of greater value. Should means be found of converting the meat into portable soup, the carcase of the sheep ought, even at its lowest value, to be considerably higher than 10s. Nothing is heard about this yet, for the country is not nearly stocked, so that the thing is not needed; but one would, *à priori*, be under the impression that there should ultimately be no insuperable difficulty in rescuing the meat from waste. It is a matter which might well attract the attention of scientific men in England. We should all be exceedingly obliged to them if they would kindly cause sheep to be as high as 15s. or 17s. seven years hence, and I can see no reason why, if the meat could be made use of, they should fall lower. In other respects, what I have written about sheep on terms is true to the present day.

years, and one can hardly suppose but that even in that advanced state of the settlement, means will not be found of investing a few thousand pounds to advantage.

The general recommendation which I receive is to buy the good-will of a run ; this cannot be done under about 100*l.* for every thousand acres. Thus, a run of 20,000 acres will be worth 2,000*l.* Still, if a man has sufficient capital to stock it well at once, it will pay him, even at this price. We will suppose the run to carry 10,000 sheep. The wool money from these should be 2,500*l.* per annum. If a man can start with 2,000 ewes, it will not be long before he finds himself worth 10,000 sheep. Then the sale of surplus stock which he has not country to feed should fetch him in fully 1,000*l.* per annum; so that, allowing the country to cost 2,000*l.*, and the sheep 2,500*l.*, and allowing 1,000*l.* for working, plant, buildings, dray, bullocks, and stores, and 500*l.* more for contingencies and expenses of the first two years, during which the run will not fully pay its own expenses—for a capital of 6,000*l.* a man may in a few years find himself possessed of something like a net income of 2,000*l.* per annum. Marvellous as all this sounds, I am assured that it is true.* On the other hand there are risks. There is the uncertainty of what will

* The above is true to the present day (August 1862), save that a higher price must be given for the good-will of a run, and that sheep are fully 30*s.* a head. Say 8,000*l.* instead of 6,000*l.*, and the rest will stand. 8,000*l.* should do the thing handsomely.

be done in the year 1870, when the runs lapse to the government. The general opinion appears to be, that they will be re-let, at a greatly advanced rent, to the present occupiers. The present rent of land is a farthing per acre for the first and second years, a halfpenny for the third, and three farthings for the fourth and every succeeding year. Most of the waste lands in the province are now paying three farthings per acre. There is the danger also of scab. This appears to depend a good deal upon the position of the run and its nature. Thus, a run situated in the plains over which sheep are being constantly driven from the province of Nelson, will be in more danger than one on the remoter regions of the back country. In Nelson there are few, if any, laws against carelessness in respect of scab. In Canterbury the laws are very stringent. Sheep have to be dipped three months before they quit Nelson, and inspected and re-dipped (in tobacco water and sulphur) on their entry into this province. Nevertheless, a single sheep may remain infected, even after this second dipping. The scab may not be apparent, but it may break out after having been a month or two in a latent state. One sheep will infect others, and the whole mob will soon become diseased; indeed, a mob is considered unsound, and compelled to be dipped, if even a single scabby sheep have joined it. Dipping is an expensive process, and if a man's sheep trespass on to his neighbour's run he has to dip his neighbour's also. Moreover, scab may break out just before or in mid-winter, when it is almost impossible, on the plains, to get firewood sufficient to boil the water and tobacco (sheep must be dipped whilst the liquid is at a temperature of not less than 90°), and when the severity of the sou'-westers renders it nearly certain that a good few sheep will be lost. Lambs, too, if there be lambs about, will be lost wholesale. If the sheep be not clean within six months after the information is laid, the sum required to be deposited with government by the owner, on the laying of such information, is forfeited. This sum is heavy, though I do not exactly know its amount. One dipping would not be ruinous, but there is always a chance of some scabby sheep having been left upon the run unmustered, and the flock thus becoming infected afresh, so that the whole work may have to be done over again. I perceive a sort of shudder to run through a sheep farmer at the very name of this disease. There are no four letters in the alphabet which he appears so mortally to detest, and with good reason.

Another mode of investment highly spoken of is that of buying land and laying it down in English grass, thus making a permanent estate of it. But I fear this will not do for me, both because it requires a large experience of things in general, which, as you well know, I do not possess, and because I should want a greater capital than would be required to start a run.

More money is sunk, and the returns do not appear to be so speedy. I cannot give you even a rough estimate of the expenses of such a plan. I will only say that I have seen gentlemen who are doing it, and who are confident of success, and these men bear the reputation of being shrewd and business-like. I cannot doubt, therefore, that it is both a good and safe investment of money. My crude notion concerning it is, that it is more permanent and less remunerative. In this I may be mistaken, but I am certain it is a thing which might very easily be made a mess of by an inexperienced person; whilst many men, who have known no more about sheep than I do, have made ordinary sheep farming pay exceedingly well. I may perhaps as well say, that land laid down in English grass is supposed to carry about five or six sheep to the acre; some say more and some less. Doubtless, somewhat will depend upon the nature of the soil, and as yet the experiment can hardly be said to have been fully tried. As for farming as we do in England, it is universally maintained that it does not pay; there seems to be no discrepancy of opinion about this. Many try it, but most men give it up. It appears as if it were only bonâ fide labouring men who can make it answer. The number of farms in the neighbourhood of Christ Church seems at first to contradict this statement; but I believe the fact to be, that these farms are chiefly in the hands of labouring men, who have made a little money, bought land, and cultivated it

themselves. These men can do well, but those who
have to buy labour cannot make it answer. The difficulty lies in the high rate of wages.

February 13.—Since my last I have been paying a
visit of a few days at Kaiapoi, and made a short trip up
to the Harewood Forest, near to which the township of
Oxford is situated. Why it should be called Oxford I
do not know.

After leaving Rangiora, which is about 8 miles from
Kaiapoi, I followed the Harewood road till it became a
mere track, then a footpath, and then dwindled away to
nothing at all. I soon found myself in the middle of
the plains, with nothing but brown tussocks of grass
before me and behind me, and on either side. The day
was rather dark, and the mountains were obliterated by
a haze. ' Oh the pleasure of the plains,' I thought to
myself; but upon my word, I think old Handel would
find but little pleasure in these. They are, in clear
weather, monotonous and dazzling; in cloudy weather
monotonous and sad; and they have little to recommend
them but the facility they afford for travelling, and the
grass which grows upon them. This, at least, was the
impression I derived from my first acquaintance with
them, as I found myself steering for the extremity of
some low downs about six miles distant. I thought
these downs would never get nearer. At length I saw
a tent-like object, dotting itself upon the plain, with
eight black mice as it were in front of it. This turned

out to be a dray, loaded with wool, coming down from the country. It was the first symptom of sheep that I had come upon, for, to my surprise, I saw no sheep upon the plains, neither did I see any in the whole of my little excursion. I am told that this disappoints most new comers. They are told that sheep farming is the great business of Canterbury, but they see no sheep; the reason of this is, partly because the runs are not yet a quarter stocked, and partly because the sheep are in mobs, and, unless one comes across the whole mob, one sees none of them. The plains, too, are so vast, that at a very short distance from the track, sheep will not be seen. When I came up to the dray, I found myself on a track, reached the foot of the downs, and crossed the little river Cust. A little river, brook, or stream, is always called a creek; nothing but the great rivers are called rivers. Now clumps of flax, and stunted groves of Ti palms and other trees, began to break the monotony of the scene. Then the track ascended the downs on the other side of the stream, and afforded me a fine view of the valley of the Cust, cleared and burnt by a recent fire, which extended for miles and miles, purpling the face of the country, up to the horizon. Rich flax and grass made the valley look promising, but on the hill the ground was stony and barren, and shabbily clothed with patches of dry and brown grass, surrounded by a square foot or so of hard ground; between the tussocks, however, there was a frequent

though scanty undergrowth which might furnish support for sheep, though it looked burnt up.

I may as well here correct an error, which I had been
under, and which you may, perhaps, have shared with
me—native grass cannot be mown.

After proceeding some few miles further, I came to a
station, where, though a perfect stranger, and at first
(at some little distance) mistaken for a Mäori, I was
most kindly treated, and spent a very agreeable evening.
The people here are very hospitable; and I have
received kindness already upon several occasions, from
persons upon whom I had no sort of claim.

Next day I went to Oxford, which lies at the foot of
the first ranges, and is supposed to be a promising
place.   Here, for the first time, I saw the bush; it was
very beautiful; numerous creepers, and a luxuriant
undergrowth among the trees, gave the forest a wholly
un-European aspect, and realised, in some degree, one's
idea of tropical vegetation.   It was full of birds that
sang loudly and sweetly.   The trees here are all evergreens, and are not considered very good for timber.
I am told that they have mostly a twist in them, and
are in other respects not first rate.

.   .   .   .

March 24.—At last I have been really in the ex-
treme back country, and positively, right up to a glacier.

As soon as I saw the mountains, I longed to get on
the other side of them, and now my wish has been
gratified.

I left Christ Church in company with a sheep farmer,
who owns a run in the back country, behind the Malvern hills, and who kindly offered to take me with him
on a short expedition he was going to make into the
remoter valleys of the island, in hopes of finding some
considerable piece of country which had not yet been
applied for.

We started February 28th, and had rather an unpleasant ride of twenty-five miles, against a very high
NW. wind. This wind is very hot, very parching, and
very violent; it blew the dust into our eyes so that we
could hardly keep them open. Towards evening, however, it somewhat moderated, as it generally does.
There was nothing of interest on the track, save a dry
river bed, through which the Waimakiriri once flowed,
but which it has long quitted. The rest of our journey
was entirely over the plains, which do not become less
monotonous upon a longer acquaintance; the mountains, however, drew slowly nearer, and by evening
were really rather beautiful. Next day we entered the
valley of the River Selwyn, or Waikitty, as it is generally called, and soon found ourselves surrounded by the
low volcanic mountains, which bear the name of the
Malvern hills. They are very like the Banks peninsula.
We dined at a station belonging to a son of the bishop's,
and after dinner made further progress into the interior.
I have very little to record, save that I was disappointed at not finding the wild plants more numerous

and more beautiful; they are few, and decidedly ugly. There is one beast of a plant they call spear grass, or spaniard, which I will tell you more about at another time. You would have laughed to have seen me on that day; it was the first on which I had the slightest occasion for any horsemanship. You know how bad a horseman I am, and can imagine that I let my companion go first in all the little swampy places and small creeks which we came across. These were numerous, and as Doctor always jumped them, with what appeared to me a jump about three times greater than was necessary, I assure you I heartily wished them somewhere else. However, I did my best to conceal my deficiency, and before night had become comparatively expert without having betrayed myself to my companion. I dare say he knew what was going on, well enough, but was too good and kind to notice it.

At night, and by a lovely clear cold moonlight, we arrived at our destination, heartily glad to hear the dogs barking and to know that we were at our journey's end. Here we were bonâ fide beyond the pale of civilisation; no boarded floors, no chairs, nor any similar luxuries; everything was of the very simplest description. Four men inhabited the hut, and their life appears a kind of mixture of that of a dog and that of an emperor, with a considerable predominance of the latter. They have no cook, and take it turn and turn to cook and wash up, two one week, and two the next. They have a good

E

garden, and gave us a capital feed of potatoes and peas, both fried together, an excellent combination. Their culinary apparatus and plates, cups, knives and forks, are very limited in number. The men are all gentlemen and sons of gentlemen, and one of them is a Cambridge man, who took a high second-class a year or two before my time. Every now and then he leaves his up-country avocations, and becomes a great gun at the college in Christ Church, examining the boys; he then returns to his shepherding, cooking, bullock-driving, &c. &c., as the case may be. I am informed that the having faithfully learned the ingenuous arts, has so far mollified his morals that he is an exceedingly humane and judicious bullock-driver. He regarded me as a somewhat despicable new-comer (at least so I imagined), and when next morning I asked where I should wash, he gave rather a French shrug of the shoulders, and said, 'The lake.' I felt the rebuke to be well merited, and that with the lake in front of the house, I should have been at no loss for the means of performing my ablutions. So I retired abashed and cleansed myself therein. Under his bed I found Tennyson's 'Idylls of the King.' So you will see that even in these out-of-the-world places people do care a little for something besides sheep. I was told an amusing story of an Oxford man shepherding down in Otago. Some one came into his hut, and, taking up a book, found it in a strange tongue, and enquired what

it was. The Oxonian (who was baking at the time)
answered that it was 'Machiavellian discourses upon the
first decade of Livy.' The wonder-stricken visitor laid
down the book and took up another, which was at any rate
written in English. This he found to be Bishop Butler's
'Analogy.' Putting it down speedily as something not
in his line, he laid hands upon a third. This proved to
be 'Patrum Apostolicorum Opera,' on which he saddled
his horse and went right away, leaving the Oxonian to
his baking. This man must certainly be considered a
rare exception. New Zealand seems far better adapted
to develope and maintain in health the physical than
the intellectual nature. The fact is, people here are
busy making money; that is the inducement which led
them to come in the first instance, and they show their
sense by devoting their energies to the work. Yet,
after all, it may be questioned whether the intellect is
not as well schooled here as at home, though in a very
different manner. Men are as shrewd and sensible as
alive to the humorous, and as hard-headed. Moreover,
there is much nonsense in the old country from which
people here are free. There is little conventionalism,
little formality, and much liberality of sentiment; very
little sectarianism, and, as a general rule, a healthy
sensible tone in conversation, which I like much. But
it does not do to speak about John Sebastian Bach's
' Fugues,' or pre-Raphaelite pictures.

To return, however, to the matter in hand. Of
course everyone at stations like the one we visited
washes his own clothes, and of course they do not use
sheets. Sheets would require far too much washing.
Red blankets are usual; white show fly-blows. The
blue-bottle flies blow among blankets that are left
lying untidily about, but if the same be neatly folded
up and present no crumpled creases, the flies will leave
them alone. It is strange, too, that, though flies
will blow a dead sheep almost immediately, they will
not touch one that is living and healthy. Coupling
their good nature in this respect with the love of neatness and hatred of untidiness which they exhibit, I
incline to think them decidedly in advance of our
English bluebottles, which they perfectly resemble in
every other respect. The English house-fly soon drives
them away, and, after the first year or two, a station is
seldom much troubled with them: so at least I am
told by many. Fly-blown blankets are all very well,
provided they have been quite dry ever since they were
blown: the eggs then come to nothing; but if the
blankets be damp, maggots make their appearance in a
few hours, and the very suspicion of them is attended
with an unpleasant creepy crawly sensation. The
blankets in which I slept at the station which I have
been describing were perfectly innocuous.

On the morning after I arrived, for the first
time in my life I saw a sheep killed. It is rather

unpleasant, but I suppose I shall get as indifferent
to it as other people are by and by. To show you
that the knives of the establishment are numbered,
I may mention that the same knife killed the sheep
and carved the mutton we had for dinner. After an
early dinner, my patron and myself started on our
journey, and after travelling for some few hours over
rather a rough country, though one which appeared to
me to be beautiful indeed, we came upon a vast river-bed,
with a little river winding about it. This is the Harpur,
a tributary of the Rakaia, and the northern branch of
that river. We were now going to follow it to its
source, in the hopes of being led by it to some saddle
over which we might cross, and come upon entirely new
ground. The river itself was very low, but the huge
and wasteful river-bed showed that there were times
when its appearance must be entirely different. We
got on to the river-bed, and, following it up for a little
way, soon found ourselves in a close valley between two
very lofty ranges, which were plentifully wooded with
black birch down to their base. There were a few
scrubby stony flats covered with Irishman and spear-
grass (Irishman is the unpleasant thorny shrub which I
saw going over the hill from Lyttelton to Christ Church)
on either side the stream; they had been entirely left
to nature, and showed me the difference between
country which had been burnt and that which is in its
natural condition. This difference is very great. The

fire dries up many swamps—at least many disappear
after country has been once or twice burnt; the
water moves more freely, unimpeded by the tangled
and decaying vegetation which accumulates round it
during the lapse of centuries, and the sun gets freer
access to the ground.   Cattle do much also : they form
tracks through swamps, and trample down the earth,
making it harder and firmer.   Sheep do much : they
convey the seeds of the best grass and tread them into
the ground.   The difference between country that
has been fed upon by any live stock, even for a single
year, and that which has never yet been stocked is very
noticeable.   If country is being burnt for the second or
third time, the fire can be crossed without any difficulty; of course it must be quickly traversed, though
indeed, on thinly-grassed land, you may take it almost
as coolly as you please.   On one of these flats, just on
the edge of the bush, and at the very foot of the mountain, we lit a fire as soon as it was dusk, and, tethering
our horses, boiled our tea and supped.   The night was
warm and quiet, the silence only interrupted by the
occasional sharp cry of a wood-hen and the rushing of
the river, whilst the ruddy glow of the fire, the sombre
forest, and the immediate foreground of our saddles
and blankets, formed a picture to me entirely new and
rather impressive.   Probably after another year or two
I shall regard camping out as the nuisance which it
really is, instead of writing about sombre forests and so

forth. Well, well, that night I thought it very fine, and so in good truth it was.

Our saddles were our pillows and we strapped our blankets round us by saddle-straps, and my companion (I believe) slept very soundly; for my part the scene was altogether too novel to allow me to sleep. I kept looking up and seeing the stars just as I was going off to sleep, and that woke me again; I had also under-estimated the amount of blankets which I should require, and it was not long before the romance of the situation wore off, and a rather chilly reality occupied its place; moreover, the flat was stony, and I was not knowing enough to have selected a spot which gave a hollow for the hip-bone. My great object, however, was to conceal my condition from my companion, for never was a freshman at Cambridge more anxious to be mistaken for a third-year man than I was anxious to become an old chum, as the colonial dialect calls a settler—thereby proving my new chumship most satisfactorily. Early next morning the birds began to sing beautifully, and the day being thus heralded, I got up, lit the fire, and set the pannikins on to boil: we then had breakfast, and broke camp. The scenery soon became most glorious, for, turning round a corner of the river, we saw a very fine mountain right in front of us. I could at once see that there was a névé near the top of it, and was all excitement. We were very anxious to know if this was the back-bone range of the island, and were hopeful that if it was we might

find some pass to the other side.   The ranges on either
hand were, as I said before, covered with bush, and these,
with the rugged Alps in front of us, made a magnificent
view.   We went on, and soon there came out a much
grander mountain—a glorious glaciered fellow—and then
came more, and the mountains closed in, and the river
dwindled and began leaping from stone to stone, and
we were shortly in scenery of the true Alpine nature—
very, very grand.   It wanted, however, a châlet or two,
or some sign of human handiwork in the foreground;
as it was, the scene was too savage.

All the time we kept looking for gold, not in a
scientific manner, but we had a kind of idea that if we
looked in the shingly beds of the numerous tributaries
to the Harpur, we should surely find either gold or
copper or something good.   So at every shingle-bed
we came to (and every little tributary had a great
shingle-bed) we lay down and gazed into the pebbles
with all our eyes.   We found plenty of stones with
yellow specks in them, but none of that rich goodly
hue which makes a man certain that what he has
found is gold.   We did not wash any of the gravel, for
we had no tin dish, neither did we know how to wash.
The specks we found were mica; but I believe I am
right in saying that there are large quantities of chromate
of iron in the ranges that descend upon the river.
We brought down several specimens, some of which we
believed to be copper, but which did not turn out to be

so. The principal rocks were a hard, grey, gritty sandstone, interwoven with thin streaks of quartz. We saw
no masses of quartz; what we found was intermixed
with sandstone, and was always in small pieces. The
sandstone, in like manner, was almost always inter-
mingled with quartz. Besides this sandstone there was
a good deal of pink and blue slate, the pink chiefly at
the top of the range, showing a beautiful colour from
the river-bed. In addition to this, there were abundance of rocks, of every gradation between sandstone and
slate—some sandstone almost slate, some slate almost
sandstone. There was also a good deal of pudding-
stone; but the bulk of the rock was this very hard, very
flinty sandstone. You know I am no geologist. I will
undertake, however, to say positively that we did not see
one atom of granite; all the mountains that I have yet
seen are either volcanic or composed of this sandstone
and slate.

When we had reached nearly the base of the mountains, we left our horses, for we could use them no
longer, and, crossing and recrossing the stream, at
length turned up through the bush to our right. This
bush, though very beautiful to look at, is composed of
nothing but the poorest black birch. We had no difficulty in getting through it, for it had no under-growth,
as the bushes on the front ranges have. I should suppose we were here between three and four thousand feet
above the level of the sea; and you may imagine that

at that altitude, in a valley surrounded by snowy ranges, vegetation would not be very luxuriant. There was sufficient wood, however, to harbour abundance of parroquets—brilliant little glossy green fellows, that shot past you now and again with a glisten in the sun, and were gone. There was a kind of dusky brownish-green parrot too, which the scientific call a Nestor. What they mean by this name I know not. To the unscientific it is a rather dirty-looking bird, with some bright red feathers under its wings. It is very tame, sits still to be petted, and screams like a real parrot. Two attended us on our ascent after leaving the bush. We threw many stones at them, and it was not their fault that they escaped unhurt.

Immediately on emerging from the bush we found all vegetation at an end. We were on the moraine of an old glacier, and saw nothing in front of us but frightful precipices and glaciers. There was a saddle, however, not above a couple of thousand feet higher. This saddle was covered with snow, and as we had neither provisions nor blankets, we were obliged to give up going to the top of it. We returned with less reluctance, from the almost absolute certainty, firstly, that we were not upon the main range ; secondly, that this saddle would only lead to the Waimakiriri, the next river above the Rakaia. Of these two points my companion was so convinced, that we did not greatly regret leaving it unexplored. Our object was commercial, and not scientific; our motive was pounds, shillings, and pence: and where this failed us, we lost all excitement and curiosity. I fear that we were yet weak enough to have a little hankering after the view from the top of the pass, but we treated such puerility with the contempt that it deserved, and sat down to rest ourselves at the foot of a small glacier. We then descended, and reached the horses at nightfall, fully satisfied that, beyond the flat beside the river-bed of the Harpur, there was no country to be had in that direction. We also felt certain that there was no pass to the west coast up that branch of the Rakaia, but that the saddle at the head of it would only lead to the Waimakiriri, and reveal the true back-bone range farther to the west. The mountains among which we had been climbing were only offsets from the main chain.

This might be shown also by a consideration of the volume of water which supplies the main streams of the Rakaia and the Waimakiriri, and comparing it with the insignificant amount which finds its way down the Harpur. · The glaciers that feed the two larger streams must be very extensive, thus showing that the highest range lies still farther to the northward and westward. The Waimakiriri is the next river to the northward of the Rakaia.

That night we camped as before, only I was more knowing, and slept with my clothes on, and found a hollow for my hip-bone, by which contrivances I slept

like a top.   Next morning, at early dawn, the scene was
most magnificent.   The mountains were pale as ghosts,
and almost sickening from their death-like whiteness.
We gazed at them for a moment or two, and then turned
to making a fire, which in the cold frosty morning was
not unpleasant.   Shortly afterwards we were again en
route for the station from which we had started.   We
burnt the flats as we rode down, and made a smoke
which was noticed between fifty and sixty miles off.   I
have seen no grander sight than the fire upon a country
which has never before been burnt, and on which there
is a large quantity of Irishman.   The sun soon loses all
brightness, and looks as though seen through smoked
glass.   The volumes of smoke are something that must
be seen to be appreciated.   The flames roar, and the
grass crackles, and every now and then a glorious lurid
flare marks the ignition of an Irishman; his dry
thorns blaze fiercely for a minute or so, and then the
fire leaves him, charred and blackened for ever.   A year
or two hence, a stiff nor'-wester will blow him over, and
he will lie there and rot, and fatten the surrounding
grass; often, however, he shoots out again from the
roots, and then he is a considerable nuisance.   On the
plains Irishman is but a small shrub, that hardly rises
higher than the tussocks; it is only in the back country
that it attains any considerable size: there its trunk is
often as thick as a man's body.

    We got back about an hour after sun-down, just as

heavy rain was coming on, and were very glad not to be again camping out, for it rained furiously and incessantly the whole night long. Next day we returned to the lower station belonging to my companion, which was as replete with European comforts as the upper was devoid of them; yet, for my part, I could live very comfortably at either.

CHAPTER V.

Ascent of the Waimakiriri — Crossing the River — Gorge —
Ascent of the Rangitata — View of M'Kenzie Plains —
M'Kenzie — Mount Cook — Ascent of the Hurunui — Col
leading to West Coast.

SINCE my last, I have made another expedition into the
back country, in the hope of finding some little run
which had been overlooked. I have been unsuccessful,
as indeed I was likely to be : still I had a pleasant
excursion, and have seen many more glaciers, and much
finer ones than on my last trip. This time I went up
the Waimakiriri by myself, and found that we had been
fully right in our supposition that the Rakaia saddles
would only lead on to that river. The main features
were precisely similar to those on the Rakaia, save that
the valley was broader, the river longer, and the mountains very much higher. I had to cross the Waimakiriri
just after a fresh, when the water was thick, and I
assure you I did not like it. I crossed it first on the
plains, where it flows between two very high terraces,
which are from half a mile to a mile apart, and of
which the most northern must be, I should think, 300
feet high. It was so steep, and so covered with stones

towards the base, and so broken with strips of shingle that had fallen over the grass, that it took me a full hour to lead my horse from the top to the bottom. I dare say my clumsiness was partly in fault; but certainly in Switzerland I never saw a horse taken down so nasty a place: and so glad was I to be at the bottom of it, that I thought comparatively little of the river, which was close at hand waiting to be crossed. From the top of the terrace I had surveyed it carefully as it lay beneath, wandering capriciously in the wasteful shingle-bed, and looking like a maze of tangled silver ribbons. I calculated how to cut off one stream after another, but I could not shirk the main stream, dodge it how I might; and when on the level of the river, I lost all my landmarks in the labyrinth of streams, and determined to cross each just above the first rapid I came to. The river was very milky, and the stones at the bottom could not be seen, except just at the edges: I do not know how I got over. I remember going in, and thinking that the horse was lifting his legs up and putting them down in the same place again, and that the river was flowing backwards. In fact I grew dizzy directly, but by fixing my eyes on the opposite bank, and leaving Doctor to manage matters as he chose, somehow or other, and much to my relief, I got to the other side. It was really nothing at all. I was wet only a little above the ankle; but it is the rapidity of the stream which makes it so unpleasant—in fact, so

positively hard to those who are not used to it. On
their few first experiences of one of these New Zealand
rivers, people dislike them extremely; they then become
very callous to them, and are as unreasonably foolhardy
as they were before timorous; then they generally get
an escape from drowning or two, or else they get
drowned in earnest. After one or two escapes their
original respect for the rivers returns, and for ever after
they learn not to play any unnecessary tricks with them.
Not a year passes but what each of them sends one or more
to his grave; yet as long as they are at their ordinary
level, and crossed with due care, there is no real danger
in them whatever. I have crossed and recrossed the
Waimakiriri so often in my late trip that I have ceased
to be much afraid of it unless it is high, and then I
assure you that I am far too nervous to attempt it.
When I crossed it first I was assured that it was not
high, but only a little full.

The Waimakiriri flows from the back country out
into the plains through a very beautiful narrow gorge.
The channel winds between wooded rocks, beneath
which the river whirls and frets and eddies most glo-
riously. Above the lower cliffs, which descend perpendicularly into the river, rise lofty mountains to an
elevation of several thousand feet: so that the scenery
here is truly fine. In the river-bed, near the gorge,
there is a good deal of lignite, and, near the Kowai, a
little tributary which comes in a few miles below the

gorge, there is an extensive bed of true and valuable coal.

The back country of the Waimakiriri is inaccessible by dray, so that all the stores and all the wool have to be packed in and packed out on horseback. This is a very great drawback, and one which is not likely to be soon removed. In winter time, also, the pass which leads into it is sometimes entirely obstructed by snow, so that the squatters in that part of the country must have a harder time of it than those on the plains. They have bush, however, and that is a very important thing.

I shall not give you any full account of what I saw as I went up the Waimakiriri, for were I to do so I should only repeat my last letter. Suffice it that there is a magnificent mountain chain of truly Alpine character at the head of the river, and that, in parts, the scenery is quite equal in grandeur to that of Switzerland, but far inferior in beauty. How one does long to see some signs of human care in the midst of the loneliness! How one would like, too, to come occasionally across some little auberge, with its vin ordinaire and refreshing fruit! These things, however, are as yet in the far future. As for *vin ordinaire*, I do not suppose that, except at Akaroa, the climate will ever admit of grapes ripening in this settlement—not that the summer is not warm enough, but because the night frosts come early, even while the days are exceedingly hot. Neither does

F

one see how these back valleys can ever become so densely peopled as Switzerland; they are too rocky and too poor, and too much cut up by river-beds.

I saw one saddle low enough to be covered with bush, ending a valley of some miles in length, through which flowed a small stream with dense bush on either side. I firmly believe that this saddle will lead to the West Coast; but as the valley was impassable for a horse, and as, being alone, I was afraid to tackle the carrying food and blankets, and to leave Doctor, who might very probably walk off whilst I was on the wrong side of the Waimakiriri, I shirked the investigation. I certainly ought to have gone up that valley. I feel as though I had left a stone unturned, and must, if all is well, at some future time take some one with me and explore it. I found a few flats up the river, but they were too small and too high up, to be worth my while to take.

April 1860.—I have made another little trip, and this time have tried the Rangitata. My companion and myself have found a small piece of country, which we have just taken up. We fear it may be snowy in winter, but the expense of taking up country is very small; and even should we eventually throw it up, the chances are that we may be able to do so with profit. We are, however, sanguine that it may be a very useful little run, but shall have to see it through next winter before we can safely put sheep upon it.

I have little to tell you concerning the Rangitata differ-

ent from what I have already written about the Waimakiriri and the Harpur. The first great interest was of
course finding the country which we took up; the next
was what I confess to the weakness of having enjoyed
much more—namely, a most magnificent view of that
most magnificent mountain, Mount Cook. It is one of
the grandest I have ever seen. I will give you a short
account of the day.

We started from a lonely valley, down which runs a
stream called Forest Creek. It is an ugly barren-look-
ing place enough — a deep valley between two high
ranges, which are not entirely clear of snow for more
than three or four months in the year. As its name
imports, it has some wood, though not much, for the
Rangitata back country is very bare of timber. We
started, as I said, from the bottom of this valley on a
clear frosty morning—so frosty that the tea-leaves in our
pannikins were frozen, and our outer blanket crisped
with frozen dew. We went up a little gorge, as narrow
as a street in Genoa, with huge black and dripping
precipices overhanging it, so as almost to shut out the
light of heaven. I never saw so curious a place in my
life. It soon opened out, and we followed up the little
stream which flowed through it. This was no easy work.
The scrub was very dense, and the rocks huge. The
spaniard 'piked us intil the bane,' and I assure you
that we were hard set to make any head-way at all. At
last we came to a waterfall, the only one worthy of the

name that I have yet seen. This 'stuck us up,' as
they say here concerning any difficulty. We managed,
however, to 'slew' it, as they, no less elegantly, say
concerning the surmounting of an obstacle. After five
hours of most toilsome climbing, we found the vegetation become scanty, and soon got on to the loose shingle
which was near the top of the range.

In seven hours from the time we started, we were on
the top. Hence we had hoped to discover some entirely
new country, but were disappointed, for we only saw
the Mackenzie Plains lying stretched out for miles away
to the southward. These plains are so called after a
notorious shepherd, who discovered them some few years
since. Keeping his knowledge to himself, he used to
steal his master's sheep and drive them quietly into his
unsuspected hiding-place. This he did so cleverly that
he was not detected until he had stolen many hundred.
Much obscurity hangs over his proceedings: it is supposed that he made one successful trip down to Otago,
through this country, and sold a good many of the sheep
he had stolen. He is a man of great physical strength,
and can be no common character; many stories are told
about him, and his fame will be lasting. He was taken
and escaped more than once, and finally was pardoned
by the Governor, on condition of his leaving New
Zealand. It was rather a strange proceeding, and I
doubt how fair to the country which he may have
chosen to honour with his presence, for I should

suppose there is hardly a more daring and dangerous rascal going. However, his boldness and skill had won him sympathy and admiration, so that I believe the pardon was rather a popular act than otherwise. To return. There we lay on the shingle-bed, at the top of the range, in the broiling noonday; for even at that altitude it was very hot, and there was no cloud in the sky and very little breeze. I saw that if we wanted a complete view we must climb to the top of a peak which, though only a few hundred feet higher than where we were lying, nevertheless hid a great deal from us. I accordingly began the ascent, having arranged with my companion that if there was country to be seen he should be called, if not, he should be allowed to take it easy. Well, I saw snowy peak after snowy peak come in view as the summit in front of me narrowed, but no mountains were visible higher or grander than what I had already seen. Suddenly, as my eyes got on a level with the top, so that I could see over, I was struck almost breathless by the wonderful mountain that burst on my sight. The effect was startling. It rose towering in a massy parallelogram, disclosed from top to bottom in the cloudless sky, far above all the others. It was exactly opposite to me, and about the nearest in the whole range. So you may imagine that it was indeed a splendid spectacle. It has been calculated by the Admiralty people at 13,200 feet, but Mr. Haast, a gentleman of high scientific attainments in the employ of Government as geological surveyor, says that it is considerably higher. For my part, I can well believe it. Mont Blanc himself is not so grand in shape, and does not look so imposing. Indeed, I am not sure that Mount Cook is not the finest in outline of all the snowy mountains that I have ever seen. It is not visible from many places on the eastern side of the island, and the front ranges are so lofty that they hide it. It can be seen from the top of Banks's Peninsula, and for a few hundred yards somewhere near Timaru, and over a good deal of the Mackenzie country ; but nowhere else on the eastern side of this settlement, unless from a great height. It is, however, well worth any amount of climbing to see. No one can mistake it. If a person says he *thinks* he has seen Mount Cook, you may be quite sure that he has not seen it. The moment it comes into sight the exclamation is, ' That is Mount Cook !'—not ' That *must* be Mount Cook !' There is no possibility of mistake. There is a glorious field for the members of the Alpine Club here. Mount Cook awaits them, and he who first scales it will be crowned with undying laurels : for my part, though it is hazardous to say this of any mountain, I do not think that any human being will ever reach its top.

I am forgetting myself into admiring a mountain which is of no use for sheep. This is wrong. A mountain here is only beautiful if it has good grass on it. Scenery is not scenery—it is ' country,' *subauditâ voce* 'sheep.' If it is good for sheep, it is beautiful, magnificent, and all the rest of it; if not, it is not worth looking at. I am cultivating this tone of mind with considerable success, but you must pardon me for an occasional outbreak of the old Adam.

Of course I called my companion up, and he agreed with me that he had never seen anything so wonderful. We got down, very much tired, a little after dark. We had had a very fatiguing day, but it was amply repaid. That night it froze pretty sharply, and our upper blankets were again stiff.

.   .   .   .

May 1860.—Not content with the little piece of country we found recently, we have since been up the Hurunui to its source, and seen the water flowing down the Teramakaw (or the 'Tether-my-cow,' as the Europeans call it). We did no good, and turned back, partly owing to bad weather, and partly from the impossibility of proceeding farther with horses. Indeed, our pack-horse had rolled over more than once, frightening us much, but fortunately escaping unhurt. The season, too, is getting too late for any long excursion. The Hurunui is not a snow river; the great range becomes much lower here, and the saddle of the Hurunui can hardly be more than 3,000 feet above the level of the sea. Vegetation is luxuriant — most abominably and unpleasantly luxuriant (for there is no getting through it)—at the very top. The reason of this is, that the nor'westers, coming heavily charged with warm moisture, deposit it on the western side of the great range, and the saddles, of course, get some of the benefit. As we were going up the river, we could see the gap at the end of it, covered with dense clouds, which were coming from the NW., and which just lipped over the saddle, and then ended. There are some beautiful lakes on the Hurunui, surrounded by lofty wooded mountains. The few Maories that inhabit this settlement travel to the west coast by way of this river. They always go on foot, and we saw several traces of their encampments— little *mimis*, as they are called — a few light sticks thrown together, and covered with grass, affording a sort of half-and-half shelter for a single individual. How comfortable!

CHAPTER VI.

I AM now going to put up a V hut on the country that
I took up on the Rangitata, meaning to hibernate there
in order to see what the place is like. I shall also build
a more permanent hut there, for I must have some one
with me, and we may as well be doing something as
nothing. I have hopes of being able to purchase some
good country in the immediate vicinity. There is a
piece on which I have my eye, and which adjoins that I
have already. There can be, I imagine, no doubt that
this is excellent sheep country ; still, I should like to see
it in winter.

.   .   .   .

June 1860.—The V hut is a *fait accompli*, if so
small an undertaking can be spoken of in so dignified a
manner. It consists of a small roof set upon the ground ;
it is a hut, all roof and no walls. I was very clumsy,
and so, in good truth, was my man. Still, at last, by

dint of perseverance, we have made it wind and water
tight. It was a job that should have taken us about a
couple of days to have done in first-rate style; as it was,
I am not going to tell you how long it *did* take. I
must certainly send the man to the right-about, but the
difficulty is to get another, for the aforesaid hut is five
and twenty miles (at the very least) from any human
habitation, so that you may imagine men do not abound.
I had two cadets with me, and must explain that a
cadet means a young fellow who has lately come out, and
who wants to see a little of up-country life. He is
neither paid nor pays. He receives his food and lodging *gratis*, but works (or is supposed to work) in order
to learn. The two who accompanied me both left me
in a very short time. I have nothing to say against
either of them; both did their best, and I am much
obliged to them for what they did, but a very few days'
experience showed me that the system is a bad one for
all the parties concerned in it. The cadet soon gets
tired of working for nothing; and, as he is not paid, it is
difficult to come down upon him. If he is good for anything, he is worth pay, as well as board and lodging. If
not worth more than these last, he is simply a nuisance,
for he sets a bad example, which cannot be checked
otherwise than by dismissal; and it is not an easy or
pleasant matter to dismiss one whose relation is rather
that of your friend than your servant. The position is
a false one, and the blame of its failure lies with the

person who takes the cadet, for either he is getting an advantage without giving its due equivalent, or he is keeping a useless man about his place, to the equal detriment both of the man and of himself. It may be said that the advantage offered to the cadet, in allowing him an insight into colonial life, is a *bonâ fide* payment for what work he may do. This is not the case; for where labour is so very valuable, a good man is in such high demand, that he may find well-paid employment directly. When a man takes a cadet's billet, it is a tolerably sure symptom that he means half-and-half work, in which case he is much worse than useless. There is, however, another alternative, which is a very different matter. Let a man pay not only for his board and lodging, but a good premium likewise, for the insight that he obtains into up-country life, then he is at liberty to work or not as he chooses; the station-hands cannot look down upon him, as they do upon the other cadet, neither, if he chooses to do nothing (which is far less likely if he is on this footing than on the other), is his example pernicious—it is well understood that he pays for the privilege of idleness, and has a perfect right to use it if he sees fit. I need not say that this last arrangement is only calculated for those who come out with money; those who have none should look out for the first employment which they feel themselves calculated for, and go in for it at once.

You may ask, What is the opening here for young

men of good birth and breeding, who have nothing but health and strength and energy for their capital? I would answer, Nothing very brilliant; still, they may be pretty sure of getting a shepherd's billet somewhere up-country, if they are known to be trustworthy. If they sustain this character, they will soon make friends, and find no great difficulty, after the lapse of a year or two, in getting an overseer's place, with from 100*l.* to 200*l.* a year, and their board and lodging. They will find plenty of good investments for the small sums which they may be able to lay by, and if they are *bonâ fide* smart men, some situation is quite sure to turn up by and by, in which they may better themselves. In fact, they are quite sure to do well in time; but time is necessary here, as well as in other places. True, less time may do here, and true also that there are more openings; but it may be questioned whether good, safe, ready-witted men will not fetch nearly as high a price in England as in any part of the world. So that, if a young and friendless lad lands here, and makes his way and does well, the chances are that he would have done well also had he remained at home. If he has money, the case is entirely changed; he can invest it far more profitably here than in England. Any merchant will give him 10 per cent. for it. Money is not to be had for less, go where you will for it; and if obtained from a merchant, his 2½ per cent. commission, repeated at intervals of six months, makes a nominal 10 per cent. into 15. I mention this to show you that, if it pays people to give this exorbitant rate of interest (and the current rate *must* be one that will pay the borrower), the means of increasing capital in this settlement are great. For young men, however, sons of gentlemen and gentlemen themselves, sheep or cattle are the most obvious and best investment. They can buy, and put out upon terms, as I have already described. They can also buy land, and let it with a purchasing clause, by which they can make first-rate interest. Thus, twenty acres cost 40*l.*; this they can let for five years, at 5*s.* an acre, the lessee being allowed to purchase the land at 5*l.* an acre in five years' time, which, the chances are, he will be both able and willing to do. Beyond sheep, cattle, and land, there are few if any investments here for gentlemen who come out with little practical experience in any business or profession, but others would turn up with time.

What I have written above refers to good men. There are many such who find the conventionalities of English life distasteful to them, who want to breathe a freer atmosphere, and yet have no unsteadiness of character or purpose to prevent them from doing well—men whose health and strength and good sense are more fully developed than delicately organised—who find head-work irksome and distressing, but who would be ready to do a good hard day's work at some physically laborious employment. If they are in earnest, they are certain to do well; if not, they had better be idle at home than here. Idle men in this country are pretty sure to take to drinking. Whether men are rich or poor, there seems to be far greater tendency towards drink here than at home; and sheep-farmers, as soon as they get things pretty straight, and can afford to leave off working themselves, are apt to turn drunkards, unless they have a taste for intellectual employments. They find time hang heavy on their hands, and, unknown almost to themselves, fall into the practice of drinking, till it becomes a habit. I am no teetotaller, and do not want to moralise unnecessarily; still it is impossible, after a few months' residence in the settlement, not to be struck with the facts I have written above.

I should be loth to advise any gentleman to come out here, unless he have either money and an average share of good sense, or else a large amount of proper self-respect and strength of purpose. If a young man goes out to friends, on an arrangement definitely settled before he leaves England, he is at any rate certain of employment and of a home upon his landing here; but if he lands friendless, or simply the bearer of a few letters of introduction, obtained from second or third hand — because his cousin knew somebody who had a friend who had married a lady whose nephew was somewhere in New Zealand — he has no very enviable look-out upon his arrival.

.   .   .   .   .   .

A short time after I got up to the Rangitata, I had occasion to go down again to Christ Church, and stayed there one day. On my return, with a companion, we were delayed two days at the Rakaia: a very heavy fresh had come down, so as to render the river impassable even in the punt. The punt can only work upon one stream; but in a heavy fresh the streams are very numerous, and almost all of them impassable for a horse without swimming him, which, in such a river as the Rakaia, is very dangerous work. Sometimes, perhaps half a dozen times in a year, the river is what is called bank and bank, that is to say, one mass of water from one side to the other. It is frightfully rapid, and as thick as pea soup. The river-bed is not far short of a mile in breadth, so you may judge of the immense volume of water that comes down it at these times. It is seldom more than three days impassable in the punt. On the third day they commenced crossing in the punt, behind which we swam our horses; since then the clouds had hung unceasingly upon the mountain ranges, and though much of what had fallen would, on the back ranges, be in all probability snow, we could not doubt but that the Rangitata would afford us some trouble, nor were we even certain about the Ashburton, a river which, though partly glacier-fed, is generally easily crossed anywhere. We found the Ashburton high, but lower than it had been; in one or two of the eleven crossing-places between our afternoon and evening resting-places we were wet up to the saddle-flaps — still we were able to proceed without any real difficulty. That night it snowed, and the next morning we started amid a heavy rain, being anxious, if possible, to make my own place that night.

Soon after we started the rain ceased, and the clouds slowly uplifted themselves from the mountain sides. We were riding through the valley that leads from the Ashburton to the upper valley of the Rangitata, and kept on the right-hand side of it. It is a long open valley, the bottom of which consists of a large swamp, from which rises terrace after terrace up the mountains on either side; the country is, as it were, crumpled up in an extraordinary manner, so that it is full of small ponds or lagoons—sometimes dry, sometimes merely swampy, now as full of water as they could be. The number of these is great; they do not, however, attract the eye, being hidden by the hillocks with which each is more or less surrounded; they vary in extent from a few square feet or yards to perhaps an acre or two, while one or two attain the dimensions of a considerable lake. There is no timber in this valley, and accordingly the scenery, though on a large scale, is neither impressive nor pleasing; the mountains are large swelling hummocks, grassed up to the summit, and though steeply declivitous, entirely destitute of precipice. Truly it is rather a dismal place on a dark day, and somewhat like the world's end which the young prince

travelled to in the story of 'Cherry, or the Frog Bride.'
The grass is coarse and cold-looking—great tufts of
what is called snow-grass, and spaniard. The first of
these grows in a clump sometimes five or six feet in
diameter and four or five feet high; sheep and cattle
pick at it when they are hungry, but seldom touch it
while they can get anything else. Its seed is like that
of oats. It is an unhappy-looking grass, if grass it be.
Spaniard, which I have mentioned before, is simply
detestable; it has a strong smell, half turpentine half
celery. It is sometimes called spear-grass, and grows
to about the size of a mole-hill, all over the back
country everywhere, as thick as mole-hills in a very
mole-hilly field at home. Its blossoms, which are green,
insignificant, and ugly, are attached to a high spike
bristling with spears pointed every way and very
acutely; each leaf terminates in a strong spear, and so
firm is it, that if you come within its reach, no amount
of clothing about the legs will prevent you from feeling
its effects. I have had my legs marked all over by it.
Horses hate the spaniard—and no wonder. In the
back country, when travelling without a track, it is
impossible to keep your horse from yawing about this
way and that to dodge it, and if he encounters three or
four of them growing together, he will jump over them
or do anything rather than walk through. A kind of
white wax, which burns with very great brilliancy,
exudes from the leaf. There are two ways in which

spaniard may be converted to some little use. The first
is in kindling a fire to burn a run: a dead flower-stalk
serves as a torch, and you can touch tussock after
tussock literally πήγη ναρθηκοπληρώτου πυρός, lighting
them at right angles to the wind. The second is purely
prospective; it will be very valuable for planting on the
tops of walls to serve instead of broken bottles: not a
cat would attempt a wall so defended.

Snow-grass, tussock grass, spaniard, rushes, swamps,
lagoons, terraces, meaningless rises and indentations
of the ground, and two great brown grassy mountains
on either side, are the principal and uninteresting
objects in the valley through which we were riding.
I despair of giving you an impression of the real
thing. It is so hard for an Englishman to divest himself, not only of hedges and ditches, and cuttings and
bridges, but of all signs of human existence whatso-
ever, that unless you were to travel in similar country
yourself, you would never understand it.

After about ten miles we turned a corner, and looked
down upon the upper valley of the Rangitata—very
grand, very gloomy, and very desolate. The river bed,
about a mile and a half broad, was now conveying a
very large amount of water to sea.

Some think that the source of the river lies many
miles higher, and that it works its way yet far back
into the mountains; but as we looked up the river bed,
we saw two large and gloomy gorges, at the end of each

of which were huge glaciers, distinctly visible to the naked eye, but through the telescope resolvable into tumbled masses of blue ice, exact counterparts of the Swiss and Italian glaciers. These are quite sufficient to account for the volume of water in the Rangitata, without going any farther.

The river had been high for many days; so high that a party of men, who were taking a dray over to a run which was then being just started on the other side (and which is now mine), had been detained camping out for ten days, and were delayed for ten days more before the dray could cross. We spent a few minutes with these men, among whom was a youth whom I had brought away from home with me, when I was starting down for Christ Church, in order that he might get some beef from P——'s and take it back again. The river had come down the evening on which we had crossed it, and so he had been unable to get the beef and himself home again.

We all wanted to get back, for home, though home be only a V hut, is worth pushing for; a little thing will induce a man to leave it, but if he is near his journey's end he will go through most places to reach it again. So we determined on going on, and after great difficulty and many turnings up one stream and down another, we succeeded in getting safely over. We were wet well over the knee, but just avoided swimming. I got into one quicksand, of which the river is full, and had to jump off my mare, but this was quite near the bank.

I had a cat on the pommel of my saddle, for the rats used to come and take the meat from off our very plates by our side. She got a sousing when the mare was in the quicksand, but I heard her purring not very long after, and was comforted. Of course she was in a bag. I do not know how it is, but men here are much fonder of cats than they are at home.

After we had crossed the river, there were many troublesome creeks yet to go through—sluggish and swampy, with bad places for getting in and out at; these, however, were as nothing in comparison with the river itself, which we all had feared more than we cared to say, and which, in good truth, was not altogether unworthy of fear.

By and by we turned up the shingly river-bed which leads to the spot on which my hut is built. The river is called Forest Creek, and, though usually nothing but a large brook, it was now high, and unpleasant from its rapidity and the large boulders over which it flows. Little by little, night and heavy rain came on, and right glad were we when we saw the twinkling light on the terrace where the hut was, and were thus assured that the Irishman, who had been left alone and without meat for the last ten days, was still in the land of the living. Two or three coo-eys soon made him aware that we were coming, and I believe he was

almost as pleased to see us as Robinson Crusoe was to
see the Spaniard who was brought over by the cannibals
to be killed and eaten. What the old Irishman had
been about during our absence I cannot say. He could
not have spent much time in eating, for there was
wonderfully little besides flour, tea, and sugar for him
to eat. There was no grog upon the establishment, so
he could not have been drinking. He had distinctly
seen my ghost two nights before. I had been coherently
drowned in the Rangitata; and when he heard us coo-
eying he was almost certain that it was the ghost again.

I had left the V hut warm and comfortable, and on my
return found it very different. I fear we had not put
enough thatch upon it, and the ten days' rain had proved
too much for it. It was now neither air-tight nor water-
tight; the floor, or rather the ground, was soaked and
soppy with mud; the nice warm snow-grass on which I
had lain so comfortably the night before I left, was muddy
and wet; altogether, there being no fire inside, the place
was as revolting-looking an affair as one would wish to
see: coming wet and cold off a journey, we had hoped
for better things. There was nothing for it but to make
the best of it, so we had tea, and fried some of the beef
—the smell of which was anything but agreeable, for
it had been lying ten days on the ground on the other
side the Rangitata, and was, to say the least, somewhat
high—and then we sat in our great-coats on four stones
round the fire, and smoked; then I baked, and one of

the cadets washed up; and then we arranged our blankets as best we could, and were soon asleep, alike unconscious of the dripping rain, which came through the roof of the hut, and of the cold raw atmosphere which was insinuating itself through the numerous crevices of the thatch.

I had brought up a tin kettle with me. This was a great comfort and acquisition, for before we had nothing larger than pint pannikins to fetch up water in from the creek; this was all very well by daylight, but in the dark the hundred yards from the hut to the creek were no easy travelling with a pannikin in each hand. The ground was very stony, and covered with burnt Irishman scrub, against which (the Irishman being black and charred, and consequently invisible in the dark) I was continually stumbling and spilling half the water. There was a terrace too, so that we seldom arrived with much more than half a pannikin, and the kettle was an immense step in advance. The Irishman called it very 'beneficial,' as he called everything that pleased him. He was a great character: he used to 'destroy' his food, not eat it. If I asked him to have any more bread or meat, he would say, with perfect seriousness, that he had 'destroyed enough this time.' He had many other quaint expressions of this sort, but they did not serve to make the hut water-tight, and I was half regretfully obliged to send him away a short time afterwards.

The winter's experience satisfied me that the country

that H—— and I had found would not do for sheep, unless worked in connection with more that was clear of snow throughout the year. As soon, therefore, as I was convinced that the adjacent country was safe, I bought it, and settled upon it in good earnest, abandoning the V hut. I did so with some regret, for we had good fare enough in it, and I rather liked it; we had only stones for seats, but we made splendid fires, and got fresh and clean snow-grass to lie on, and dried the floor with wood-ashes. Then we confined the snow-grass within certain limits by means of a couple of poles laid upon the ground and fixed into their places with pegs; then we put up several slings to hang our saddle-bags, tea, sugar, salt, bundles, &c.; then we made a horse for the saddles—four riding-saddles and a pack-saddle—and underneath this went our tools at one end and our culinary utensils, limited but very effective, at the other. Having made it neat we kept it so, and of a night it wore an aspect of comfort quite domestic, even to the cat, which would come in through a hole left in the thatched door for her especial benefit, and purr a regular hurricane. We blessed her both by day and by night, for we saw no rats after she came; and great excitement prevailed when, three weeks after her arrival, she added a litter of kittens to our establishment.

CHAPTER VII.

I COMPLETED the loading of my dray on a Tuesday
afternoon in the early part of October, 1860, and determined on making Main's accommodation-house that
night. Of the contents of the dray I need hardly
speak, though perhaps a full enumeration of them
might afford no bad index to the requirements of a
station; they are more numerous than might at first be
supposed—rigidly useful and rarely if ever ornamental.

Flour, tea, sugar, tools, household utensils few and
rough, a plough and harrows, doors, windows, oats and
potatoes for seed, and all the usual denizens of a
kitchen garden; these, with a few private effects,
formed the main bulk of the contents, amounting to
about a ton and a half in weight. I had only six
bullocks, but these were good ones, and worth many a
team of eight; a team of eight will draw from two to
three tons along a pretty good road. Bullocks are very
scarce here; none are to be got under twenty pounds,

while thirty pounds is no unusual price for a good harness bullock. They can do much more in harness than in bows and yokes, but the expense of harness and the constant disorder into which it gets, render it cheaper to use more bullocks in the simpler tackle. Each bullock has its name, and knows it as well as a dog does his. There is generally a tinge of the comic in the names given to them. Many stations have a small mob of cattle from whence to draw their working bullocks, so that a few more or a few less makes little or no difference. They are not fed with corn at accommodation-houses, as horses are ; when their work is done, they are turned out to feed till dark, or till eight or nine o'clock. A bullock fills himself, if on pretty good feed, in about three or three and a half hours ; he then lies down till very early morning, at which time the chances are ten to one that, awakening refreshed and strengthened, he commences to stray back along the way he came, or in some other direction ; accordingly, it is a common custom, about eight or nine o'clock, to yard one's team, and turn them out with the first daylight for another three or four hours' feed. Yarding bullocks is, however, a bad plan. They do their day's work of from fifteen to twenty miles, or sometimes more, at one spell, and travel at the rate of from two and a half to three miles an hour.

The road from Christ Church to Main's is metalled for about four and a half miles ; there are fences and fields on both sides, either laid down in English grass or sown with grain; the fences are chiefly low ditch and bank planted with gorse, rarely with quick, the scarcity of which detracts from the resemblance to English scenery which would otherwise prevail. The copy, however, is slatternly compared with the original; the scarcity of timber, the high price of labour, and the pressing urgency of more important claims upon the time of the small agriculturist, prevent him, for the most part, from attaining the spic and span neatness of an English homestead. Many makeshifts are necessary; a broken rail or gate is mended with a piece of flax, so, occasionally, are the roads. I have seen the government roads themselves being repaired with no other material than stiff tussocks of grass, flax, and rushes: this is bad, but to a certain extent necessary, where there is so much to be done and so few hands and so little money with which to do it.

After getting off the completed portion of the road, the track commences along the plains unassisted by the hand of man. Before one, and behind one, and on either hand, waves the yellow tussock upon the stony plain, interminably monotonous. On the left, as you go southward, lies Banks's Peninsula, a system of submarine volcanoes culminating in a flattened dome, a little more than 3,000 feet high. Cook called it Banks's Island, either because it was an island in his day, or because no one, to look at it, would imagine that it was anything else. Most probably the latter is the true reason; though

as the land is being raised by earthquakes, it is just
possible that the peninsula may have been an island in
Cook's days, for the foot of the peninsula is very little
above the sea-level. It is indeed true that the harbour
of Wellington has been raised some feet since the
foundation of the settlement, but the opinion here is
general, that it must have been many centuries since
the peninsula was an island.

On the right, at a considerable distance, rises the
long range of mountains which the inhabitants of
Christ Church suppose to be the back-bone of the
island, and which they call the Snowy Range. The real
axis of the island, however, lies much farther back, and
between it and the range now in sight, the land has no
rest, but is continually steep up and steep down, as if
Nature had determined to try how much mountain she
could place upon a given space; she had, however, still
some regard for utility, for the mountains are rarely
precipitous—very steep, often rocky and shingly when
they have attained a great elevation, but seldom, if ever,
until in immediate proximity to the west coast range,
abrupt like the descent from the top of Snowdon towards
Capel Curig or the precipices of Clogwyn du'r arddu.
The great range is truly Alpine, and the front range
occasionally reaches an altitude of nearly 7,000 feet.

The result of this absence of precipice is, that there are
no waterfalls in the front ranges and few in the back,
and these few very insignificant as regards the volume

of the water.   In Switzerland one has the falls of the
Rhine, of the Aar, the Giesbach, the Staubach, and
cataracts great and small innumerable; here there is
nothing of the kind, quite as many large rivers, but few
waterfalls, to make up for which the rivers run with
an almost incredible fall.   Mount Peel is twenty-five
miles from the sea, and the river-bed of the Rangitata underneath that mountain is 800 feet above
the sea line, the river running in a straight course
though winding about in its wasteful river-bed.   To all
appearance it is running through a level plain.   Of the
remarkable gorges through which each river finds its
way out of the mountains into the plains, I must speak
when I take my dray through the gorge of the Ashburton, though this is the least remarkable of them all;
in the mean time I must return to the dray on its way
to Main's, although I see another digression awaiting
me as soon as I have got it two miles ahead of its
present position.

It is tedious work keeping constant company with the
bullocks; they travel so slowly.   Let us linger behind and
sun ourselves upon a tussock or a flax bush, and let them
travel on until we catch them up again.

They are now going down into an old river-bed
formerly tenanted by the Waimakiriri, which then
flowed into Lake Ellesmere, ten or a dozen miles south
of Christ Church, and which now enters the sea at
Kaiapoi, twelve miles north of it; besides this old

channel, it has others which it has discarded with fickle caprice for the one in which it happens to be flowing at present, and which there appears some reason for thinking it is soon going to tire of. If it eats about a hundred yards more of its gravelly bank in one place, the river will find an old bed several feet lower than its present; this bed will conduct it into Christ Church. Government had put up a wooden defence, at a cost of something like ·£2,000, but there was no getting any firm starting-ground, and a few freshes carried embankment, piles, and all away, and ate a large slice off the bank into the bargain; there is nothing for it but to let the river have its own way. Every fresh changes every ford, and to a certain extent alters every channel; after any fresh the river may shift its course directly on to the opposite side of its bed, and leave Christ Church in undisturbed security for centuries; or again, any fresh may render such a shift in the highest degree improbable, and sooner or later seal the fate of our metropolis. At present no one troubles his head much about it, although a few years ago there was a regular panic upon the subject.

These old river channels, or at any rate channels where portions of the rivers have at one time come down, are everywhere about the plains, but the nearer you get to a river the more you see of them; on either side the Rakaia, after it has got clear of the gorge, you find channel after channel, now completely grassed over for some miles, betraying the action of river water as plainly as possible. The rivers after leaving their several gorges lie, as it were, on the highest part of a huge fanlike delta, which radiates from the gorge down to the sea; the plains are almost entirely, for many miles on either side the rivers, composed of nothing but stones, all betraying the action of water. These stones are so closely packed, that at times one wonders how the tussocks and fine sweet undergrowth can force their way up through them, and even where the ground is free from stones at the surface, I am sure that at a little distance below stones would be found packed in the same way. One cannot take one's horse out of a walk in many parts of the plains when off the track—I mean, one cannot without doing violence to old-world notions concerning horses' feet.

I said the rivers lie on the highest part of the delta; not always the highest, but seldom the lowest. There is reason to believe that in the course of centuries they oscillate from side to side. For instance, four miles north of the Rakaia there is a terrace some twelve or fourteen feet high; the water in the river is nine feet above the top of this terrace. To the eye of the casual observer there is no perceptible difference between the levels, still the difference exists and has been measured. I am no geologist myself, but have been informed of this by one who is in the Government Survey Office, and upon whose authority I can rely.

The general opinion is that the Rakaia is now tending rather to the northern side. A fresh comes down upon a crumbling bank of sand and loose shingle with incredible force, tearing it away hour by hour in ravenous bites. In fording the river one crosses now a considerable stream on the northern side, where four months ago there was hardly any; while after one has done with the water part of the story, there remains a large extent of river-bed, in the process of gradually being covered with cabbage-trees, flax, tussock, Irishman, and other plants and evergreens; yet after one is once clear of the blankets (so to speak) of the river-bed, the traces of the river are no fresher on the southern than on the northern side, even if so fresh.

The plains, at first sight, would appear to have been brought down by the rivers from the mountains. The stones upon them are all water-worn, and they are traversed by a great number of old water-courses, all tending more or less from the mountains to the sea. How, then, are we to account for the deep and very wide channels cut by the rivers?—for channels, it may be, more than a mile broad, and flanked on either side by steep terraces, which, near the mountains, are several feet high? If the rivers cut these terraces, and made these deep channels, the plains must have been there already for the rivers to cut them. It must be remembered that I write without any scientific knowledge.

How, again, are we to account for the repetition of

the phenomenon exhibited by the larger rivers, in every tributary, small or great, from the glaciers to the sea? They are all as like as pea to pea in principle, though of course varying in detail. Yet every trifling water-course, as it emerges from mountainous to level ground, presents the same phenomena, namely, a large gully, far too large for the water which could ever have come down it, gradually widening out, and then disappearing. The general opinion here among the reputed cognoscenti is, that all these gullies were formed in the process of the gradual upheaval of the island from the sea, and that the plains were originally sea-bottoms, slowly raised, and still slowly raising themselves. Doubtless, the rivers brought the stones down, but they were deposited in the sea.

The terraces, which are so abundant all over the back country, and which rise, one behind another, to the number, it may be, of twenty or thirty, with the most un-picturesque regularity (on my run there are fully twenty), are supposed to be elevated sea-beaches. They are to be seen even as high as four or five thousand feet above the level of the sea, and I doubt not that a geologist might find traces of them higher still.

Therefore, though, when first looking at the plains and river-bed flats which are so abundant in the back coun-try, one might be inclined to think that no other agent than the rivers themselves had been at work, and though, when one sees the delta below, and the empty

gully above, like a minute-glass after the egg has been
boiled—the top glass empty of the sand, and the bottom
glass full of it—one is tempted to rest satisfied; yet
when we look closer, we shall find that more is wanted
in order to account for the phenomena exhibited, and
the geologists of the island supply that more, by means
of upheaval.

I pay the tribute of a humble salaam to science, and
return to my subject.

We crossed the old river-bed of the Waimakiriri, and
crawled slowly on to Main's, through the descending
twilight. One sees Main's about six miles off, and
it appears to be about six hours before one reaches it.
A little hump for the house, and a longer hump for the
stables.

The tutu not having yet begun to spring, I yarded
my bullocks at Main's. This demands explanation.
Tutu is a plant which dies away in the winter, and
shoots up anew from the old roots in spring, growing
from six inches to two or three feet in height, sometimes
even to five or six. It is of a rich green colour, and
presents, at a little distance, something the appearance
of myrtle. On its first coming above the ground, it
resembles asparagus. I have seen three varieties of it,
though I am not sure whether two of them may not be
the same, varied somewhat by soil and position. The
third grows only in high situations, and is unknown upon
the plains ; it has leaves very minutely subdivided,

H

and looks like a fern, but the blossom and seed are nearly identical with the other varieties. The peculiar property of the plant is, that though highly nutritious both for sheep and cattle when eaten upon a tolerably full stomach, it is very fatal upon an empty one. Sheep and cattle eat it to any extent, and with perfect safety, when running loose on their pasture, because they are then always pretty full; but take the same sheep and yard them for some few hours, or drive them so that they cannot feed, then turn them into tutu, and the result is, that they are immediately attacked with apoplectic symptoms, and die unless promptly bled. Nor does bleeding by any means always save them. The worst of it is, that when empty they are keenest after it, and nab it in spite of one's most frantic appeals, both verbal and flagellatory. Some say that tutu acts like clover, and blows out the stomach, so that death ensues. The seed-stones, however, contained in the dark pulpy berry, are poisonous to man, and superinduce apoplectic symptoms. The berry (about the size of a small currant) is rather good, though (like all the New Zealand berries) insipid, and is quite harmless if the stones are not swallowed. Tutu grows chiefly on and in the neighbourhood of sandy river-beds, but occurs more or less all over the settlement, and causes considerable damage every year. Horses won't touch it.

As, then, my bullocks could not get tuted on being turned out empty, I yarded them. The next day we made thirteen miles over the plains to the Waikitty (written Waikirikiri) or Selwyn. Still the same monotonous plains, the same interminable tussock, dotted with the same cabbage-trees.

On the morrow, ten more monotonous miles to the banks of the Rakaia. This river is one of the largest in the province, second only to the Waitangi. It contains about as much water as the Rhone above Martigny, perhaps even more, but it rather resembles an Italian than a Swiss river. With due care, it is fordable in many places, though very rarely so when occupying a single channel. It is, however, seldom found in one stream, but flows, like the rest of these rivers, with alternate periods of rapid and comparatively smooth water every few yards. The place to look for a ford is just above a spit where the river forks into two or more branches; there is generally here a bar of shingle with shallow water, while immediately below, in each stream, there is a dangerous rapid. A very little practice and knowledge of each river will enable a man to detect a ford at a glance. These fords shift every fresh. In the Waimakiriri or Rangitata, they occur every quarter of a mile or less; in the Rakaia, you may go three or four miles for a good one. During a fresh, the Rakaia is not fordable, at any rate, no one ought to ford it; but the two first-named rivers may be crossed, with great care, in pretty heavy freshes, without the water going higher than the knees of the rider. It is always, however, an unpleasant task to cross a river when full, without a thorough previous acquaintance with it; then, a glance at the colour and consistency of the water will give a good idea whether the fresh is coming down, at its height, or falling. When the ordinary volume of the stream is known, the height of the water can be estimated at a spot never before seen with wonderful correctness. The Rakaia sometimes comes down with a run—a wall of water two feet high, rolling over and over, rushes down with irresistible force. I know a gentleman who had been looking at some sheep upon an island in the Rakaia, and, after finishing his survey, was riding leisurely to the bank on which his house was situated. Suddenly, he saw the river coming down upon him in the manner I have described, and not more than two or three hundred yards off. By a forcible application of the spur, he was enabled to reach *terra-firma*, just in time to see the water sweeping with an awful roar over the spot that he had been traversing not a second previously. This is not frequent : a fresh generally takes four or five hours to come down, and from two days to a week, ten days, or a fortnight, to subside again.

If I were to speak of the rise of the Rakaia, or rather of the numerous branches which form it; of their vast and wasteful beds; the glaciers that they spring from, one of which comes down half-way across the river-bed (thus tending to prove that the glaciers are descending, for the river-bed is both *above* and *below* the glacier); of the wonderful gorge with its terraces rising shelf upon shelf, like fortifications, many hundred feet above the river; the crystals found there, and the wild pigs—I should weary the reader too much, and fill half a volume: the bullocks must again claim our attention, and I unwillingly revert to my subject.

On the night of our arrival at the Rakaia I did not yard the bullocks, as they seemed inclined to stay quietly with some others that were about the place; next morning they were gone. Were they up the river, or down the river, across the river, or gone back? You are at Cambridge, and have lost your bullocks. They were bred in Yorkshire, but have been used a good deal in the neighbourhood of Dorchester, and may have consequently made in either direction; they may, however, have worked down the Cam, and be in full feed for Lynn; or, again, they may be snugly stowed away in a gully half-way between the Fitzwilliam Museum and Trumpington. You saw a mob of cattle feeding quietly about Madingley on the preceding evening, and they may have joined in with these; or were they attracted by the fine feed in the neighbourhood of Cherryhinton? Where shall you go to look for them?

Matters in reality, however, are not so bad as this. A bullock cannot walk without leaving a track, if the ground he travels on is capable of receiving one. Again, if he does not know the country in advance of him, the chances are strong that he has gone back the way he came; he will travel in a track if he happens to light on one; he finds it easier going. Animals are cautious in proceeding onwards when they do n't know the ground. They have ever a lion in their path until they know it, and have found it free from beasts of prey. If, however, they have been seen heading decidedly in any direction over-night, in that direction they will most likely be found sooner or later. Bullocks cannot go long without water. They will travel to a river, then they will eat, drink, and be merry, and during that period of fatal security they will be caught. Ours had gone back ten miles, to the Waikitty; we soon obtained clues as to their whereabouts, and had them back again in time to proceed on our journey. The river being very low, we did not unload the dray and put the contents across in the boat, but drove the bullocks straight through. Eighteen weary monotonous miles over the same plains, covered with the same tussock grass, and dotted with the same cabbage-trees. The mountains, however, grew gradually nearer, and Banks's peninsula dwindled perceptibly. That night we made Mr. M——'s station, and were thankful.

Again we did not yard the bullocks, and again we lost them. They were only five miles off, but we did not find them till afternoon, and lost a day. As they had travelled in all nearly forty miles, I had had mercy upon them, intending that they should fill themselves well during the night, and be ready for a long pull next day. Even the merciful man himself, however, would except a working bullock from the beasts who have any claim upon his good feeling. Let him go straining his eyes examining every dark spot in a circumference many long miles in extent. Let him gallop a couple of miles in this direction and the other, and discover that he has only been lessening the distance between himself and a group of cabbage-trees; let him feel the word 'bullock' eating itself in indelible characters into his heart, and he will refrain from mercy to working bullocks as long as he lives. But as there are few positive pleasures equal in intensity to the negative one of release from pain, so it is when at last a group of six oblong objects, five dark and one white, appears in remote distance, distinct and unmistakable. Yes, they are our bullocks; a sigh of relief follows, and we drive them sharply home, gloating over their distended tongues and slobbering mouths. If there is one thing a bullock hates worse than another, it is being driven too fast. His heavy lumbering carcase is mated with a no less lumbering soul. He is a good, slow, steady, patient slave if you let him take his own time about it; but do n't hurry him. He has played a very important part in the advancement of civilisation and the developement of the resources of the world, a part which the more fiery horse could not have played; let us then bear with his heavy trailing gait and uncouth movements; only next time we will keep him tight, even though he starve for it. If bullocks be invariably driven sharply back to the dray, whenever they have strayed from it, they will soon learn not to go far off, and will be cured even of the most inveterate vagrant habits.

Now we follow up one branch of the Ashburton, and commence making straight for the mountains; still, however, we are on the same monotonous plains, and crawl our twenty miles with very few objects that can possibly serve as landmarks. It is wonderful how small an object gets a name in the great dearth of features. Cabbage-tree hill, half-way between Main's and the Waikitty, is an almost imperceptible rise some ten yards across and two or three feet high: the cabbage-trees have disappeared. Between the Rakaia and Mr. M——'s station is a place they call the half-way gully, but it is neither a gully nor half-way, being only a grip in the earth, causing no perceptible difference in the level of the track, and extending but a few yards on either side of it. So between Mr. M——'s and the next halting-place (save two sheep-stations) I remember nothing but a rather curiously shaped gowai-tree, and a dead bullock, that can form miles-stones, as it were, to mark progress. Each person, however, for himself makes innumerable ones, such as where one peak in the mountain range goes behind another, and so on.

In the small river Ashburton, or rather in one of its most trivial branches, we had a little misunderstanding with the bullocks; the leaders, for some reason best known to themselves, slewed sharply round, and tied themselves into an inextricable knot with the polars, while the body bullocks, by a manœuvre not unfrequent, shifted, or as it is technically termed slipped, the yoke under their necks, and the bows over; the off bullock turning upon the near side, and the near bullock upon the off. By what means they do this I cannot explain, but believe it would make a conjurer's fortune in England. How they got the chains between their legs and how they kicked to liberate themselves, how we abused them, and, finally, unchaining them, set them right, I need not here particularise; we finally triumphed, but this delay caused us not to reach our destination till after dark.

Here the good woman of the house took us into her confidence in the matter of her corns, from the irritated condition of which she argued that bad weather was about to ensue. The next morning, however, we started anew, and, after about three or four miles, entered the valley of the south and larger Ashburton, bidding adieu to the plains completely.

And now that I approach the description of the gorge, I feel utterly unequal to the task, not because the scene is awful or beautiful, for in this respect the gorge of the Ashburton is less remarkable than most, but because the subject of gorges is replete with difficulty, and I have never heard a satisfactory explanation of the pheno-

mena they exhibit. It is not, however, my province to
attempt this. I must content myself with narrating
what I see.

First, there is the river, flowing very rapidly upon a
bed of large shingle, with alternate rapids and smooth
places, constantly forking and constantly reuniting
itself like tangled skeins of silver ribbon surrounding
lozenge-shaped islets of sand and gravel. On either side
is a long flat composed of shingle similar to the bed of
the river itself, but covered with vegetation, tussock, and
scrub, with fine feed for sheep or cattle among the burnt
Irishman thickets. The flat is some half-mile broad on
each side the river, narrowing as the mountains draw in
closer upon the stream. It is terminated by a steep
terrace. Twenty or thirty feet above this terrace is
another flat, we will say semicircular, for I am gene-
ralising, which again is surrounded by a steeply-sloping
terrace like an amphitheatre; above this another flat,
receding still farther back, perhaps half-a-mile in
places, perhaps almost close above the one below it;
above this another flat, receding farther, and so on,
until the level of the plain proper, or highest flat, is
several hundred feet above the river. I have not seen
a single river in Canterbury which is not more or less
terraced even below the gorge. The angle of the terrace is always very steep: I seldom see one less than
45°. One always has to get off and lead one's horse
down, except an artificial cutting has been made, or

advantage can be taken of some gully that descends into the flat below. Tributary streams are terraced in like manner on a small scale, while even the mountain creeks repeat the phenomena in miniature : the terraces being always highest where the river emerges from its gorge, and slowly dwindling down as it approaches the sea, till finally, instead of the river being many hundred feet below the level of the plains, as is the case at the foot of the mountains, the plains near the sea are considerably below the water in the river, as on the north side of the Rakaia, before described.

Our road lay up the Ashburton, which we had repeatedly to cross and recross.

A dray going through a river is a pretty sight enough when you are utterly unconcerned in the contents thereof; the rushing water stemmed by the bullocks and the dray, the energetic appeals of the driver to Tommy or Nobbler to lift the dray over the large stones in the river, the creaking dray, the cracking whip, form a *tout ensemble* rather agreeable than otherwise. But when the bullocks, having pulled the dray into the middle of the river, refuse entirely to pull it out again ; when the leaders turn sharp round and look at you, or stick their heads under the bellies of the polars ; when the gentle pats on the forehead with the stock of the whip prove unavailing, and you are obliged to have recourse to strong measures, it is less agreeable: especially if the animals turn just after having got your dray half-way up the bank, and twisting it round upon a steeply-inclined surface, throw the centre of gravity far beyond the base: over goes the dray into the water. Alas my sugar! my tea! my flour! my crockery! It is all over—drop the curtain.

I beg to state my dray did not upset this time, though the centre of gravity fell far without the base: what Newton says on that subject is erroneous; so are those illustrations of natural philosophy, in which a loaded dray is represented as necessarily about to fall, because a dotted line from the centre of gravity falls outside the wheels. It takes a great deal more to upset a well-loaded dray than one would have imagined, although sometimes the most unforeseen trifle will effect it. Possibly the value of the contents may have something to do with it; but my ideas are not yet fully formed upon the subject.

We made about seventeen miles and crossed the river ten times, so that the bullocks, which had never before been accustomed to river-work, became quite used to it, and manageable, and have continued so ever since.

We halted for the night at a shepherd's hut: awakening out of slumber I heard the fitful gusts of violent wind come puff, puff, buffet, and die away again; nor'-wester all over. I went out and saw the unmistakable north-west clouds tearing away in front of the moon. I remembered Mrs. W——'s corns, and anathematised them in my heart.

It may be imagined that I turned out of a comfortable bed, slipped on my boots, and then went out; no such thing: we were all lying in our clothes with one blanket between us and the bare floor—our heads pillowed on our saddle-bags.

The next day we made only three miles to Mr. P——'s station. There we unloaded the dray, greased it, and restored half the load, intending to make another journey for the remainder, as the road was very bad.

One dray had been over the ground before us. That took four days to do the first ten miles, and then was delayed several weeks on the bank of the Rangitata by a series of very heavy freshes, so we determined on trying a different route: we got farther on our first day than our predecessor had done in two, and then Possum, one of the bullocks, lay down (I am afraid he had had an awful hammering in a swampy creek where he had stuck for two hours), and would not stir an inch; so we turned them all adrift with their yokes on (had we taken them off we could not have yoked them up again), whereat Possum began feeding in a manner which plainly showed that there had not been much amiss with him. But during the interval that elapsed between our getting into the swampy creek and getting out of it a great change had come over the weather. While poor Possum was being chastised I had been reclining on the bank hard by, and occasionally interced-

ing for the unhappy animal, the men were all at him
(but what is one to do if one's dray is buried nearly to
the axle in a bog, and Possum won't pull?); so I was
taking it easy, without coat or waistcoat, and even then
feeling as if no place could be too cool to please me,
for the nor'-wester was still blowing strong and intensely
hot, when suddenly I felt a chill, and looking at the
lake below saw that the white-headed waves had changed
their direction, and that the wind had chopped round
to sou'-west.

We left the dray and went on some two or three
miles on foot for the purpose of camping where there
was firewood. There was a hut, too, in the place for
which we were making. It was not yet roofed, and
had neither door nor window; but as it was near
firewood and water we made for it, had supper, and
turned in.

In the middle of the night some one, poking his nose
out of his blanket, informed us that it was snowing,
and in the morning we found it continuing to do so,
with a good sprinkling on the ground. We thought
nothing of it, and, returning to the dray, found the
bullocks, put them to, and started on our way; but
when we came above the gully, at the bottom of which
the hut lay, we were obliged to give in. There was a
very bad creek, which we tried in vain for an hour or so
to cross. The snow was falling very thickly, and driving
right into the bullocks' faces. We were all very cold

and weary, and determined to go down to the hut again,
expecting fine weather in the morning. We carried
down a kettle, a camp oven, some flour, tea, sugar, and
salt beef; also a novel or two, and the future towels of
the establishment which wanted hemming; also the two
cats. Thus equipped we went down the gulley, and got
back to the hut about three o'clock in the afternoon.
The gulley sheltered us, and there the snow was kind
and warm, though bitterly cold on the terrace. We
threw a few burnt Irishman sticks across the top of the
walls, and put a couple of counterpanes over them,
thus obtaining a little shelter near the fire. The snow
inside the hut was about six inches deep, and soon
became sloppy, so that at night we preferred to make a
hole in the snow and sleep outside.

The fall continued all that night, and in the morning
we found ourselves thickly covered. It was still snowing hard, so there was no stirring. We read the novels,
hemmed the towels, smoked, and took it philosophically.
There was plenty of firewood to keep us warm. By
night the snow was fully two feet thick everywhere, and
in the drifts five and six feet. I determined that we
would have some grog, and had no sooner hinted the
bright idea than two volunteers undertook the rather
difficult task of getting it. The terrace must have been
150 feet above the hut; it was very steep, intersected
by numerous gullies filled with deeply drifted snow;
from the top it was yet a full quarter of a mile to

the place where we had left the dray. Still the brave fellows, inspired with hope, started in full confidence, while we put our kettle on the fire and joyfully awaited their return. They had been gone at least two hours, and we were getting fearful that they had broached the cask and helped themselves too liberally on the way, when they returned in triumph with the two-gallon keg, vowing that never in their lives before had they worked so hard. How unjustly we had suspected them will appear in the sequel.

Great excitement prevailed over drawing the cork. It was fast; it broke the point of some one's knife. 'Shove it in,' said I, breathless with impatience; no—no—it yielded, and shortly afterwards, giving up all opposition, came quickly out. A tin pannikin was produced. With a gurgling sound out flowed the precious liquid. 'Halloa!' said one; 'it 's not brandy, it 's port wine.' 'Port wine!' cried another; 'it smells more like rum.' I voted for its being claret; another moment however settled the question, and established the contents of the cask as being excellent vinegar. The two unfortunate men had brought the vinegar keg instead of the brandy.

The rest may be imagined. That night, however, two of us were attacked with diarrhœa, and the vinegar proved of great service, for vinegar and water is an admirable remedy for this complaint.

The snow continued till afternoon the next day. It

then sulkily ceased, and commenced thawing. At night it froze very hard indeed, and the next day a nor'-wester sprang up which made the snow disappear with the most astonishing rapidity. Not having then learnt that no amount of melting snow will produce any important effect upon the river, and fearing that it might rise, we determined to push on: but this was as yet impossible. Next morning, however, we made an early start, and got triumphantly to our journey's end at about half-past ten o'clock. My own country, which lay considerably lower, was entirely free of snow, while we learnt afterwards that it had never been deeper than four inches.

CHAPTER VIII.

Taking up the Run — Hut within the Boundary — Land
Regulations — Race to Christ Church — Contest for Priority
of Application — Successful Issue—Winds and their Effects —
Their conflicting Currents — Sheep crossing the River.

THERE was a little hut on my run built by another
person, and tenanted by his shepherd. G—— had an
application for 5,000 acres in the same block of country
with mine, and as the boundaries were uncertain
until the whole was surveyed, and the runs definitely
marked out on the government maps, he had placed his
hut upon a spot that turned out eventually not to
belong to him. I had waited to see how the land was
allotted before I took it up. Knowing the country well,
and finding it allotted to my satisfaction, I made my
bargain on the same day that the question was settled.
I took a tracing from the government map up with me,
and we arrived on the run about a fortnight after the
allotment. It was necessary for me to wait for this, or
I might have made the same mistake which G—— had
done. His hut was placed where it was now of no use
to him whatever, but on the very site on which I had
myself intended to build. It is beyond all possibility

of doubt upon my run; but G—— is a very difficult man to deal with, and I have had a hard task to get rid of him. To allow him to remain where he was was not to be thought of: but I was perfectly ready to pay him for his hut (such as it is) and his yard. Knowing him to be at P——'s, I set the men to their contract, and went down next day to see him and to offer him any compensation for the loss of his hut which a third party might arrange. I could do nothing with him; he threatened fiercely, and would hear no reason. My only remedy was to go down to Christ Church at once and buy the freehold of the site from the government.

The Canterbury regulations concerning the purchase of waste lands from the crown are among the very best existing. They are all free to any purchaser with the exception of a few government reserves for certain public purposes, as railway-township reserves, and so forth. Every run-holder has a preemptive right over 250 acres round his homestead, and 50 acres round any other buildings he may have upon his run. He must register this right, or it is of no avail. By this means he is secured from an enemy buying up his homestead without his previous knowledge. Whoever wishes to purchase a sheep farmer's homestead must first give him a considerable notice, and then can only buy if the occupant refuses to do so at the price of 2l. an acre. Of course the occupant would *not* refuse, and the thing is consequently never attempted. All the rest, however, of any man's run is open to purchase at the rate of 2*l*. per acre. This price is sufficient to prevent monopoly, and yet not high enough to interfere with the small capitalist. The sheep farmer cannot buy up his run and stand in the way of the developement of the country, and at the same time he is secured from the loss of it through others buying, because the price is too high to make it worth a man's while to do so when so much better investments are still open. On the plains, however, many run-holders are becoming seriously uneasy even at the present price, and blocks of 1,000 acres are frequently bought with a view to their being fenced in and laid down in English grasses. In the back country this has not yet commenced, nor is it likely to do so for many years.

But to return. Firstly, G—— had not registered any preemptive right, and, secondly, if he had it would have been worthless, because his hut was situated on my run and not on his own. I was sure that he had not bought the freehold; I was also certain that he meant to buy it. So, well knowing there was not a moment to lose, I went towards Christ Church the same afternoon, and supped at a shepherd's hut three miles lower down, and intended to travel quietly all night.

The Ashburton, however, was heavily freshed, and the night was pitch dark. After crossing and re-crossing it four times I was afraid to go on, and camping down, waited for daylight. Resuming my journey with early dawn, I had not gone far when, happening to turn round, I saw a man on horseback about a quarter of a mile behind me. I knew at once that this was G——, and letting him come up with me, we rode for some miles together, each of us of course well aware of the other's intentions, but too politic to squabble about them when squabbling was no manner of use. It was then early on the Wednesday morning, and the Board sat on the following day. A book is kept at the Land-Office called the application-book, in which anyone who has business with the Board enters his name, and his case is attended to in the order in which his name stands. The race between G—— and myself was as to who should first get his name down in this book, and secure the ownership of the hut by purchasing the freehold of twenty acres round it. We had nearly a hundred miles to ride; the office closed at four in the afternoon, and I knew that G—— could not possibly be in time for that day; I had therefore till ten o'clock on the following morning, that is to say, about twenty-four hours from the time we parted company. Knowing that I could be in town by that time, I took it easily, and halted for breakfast at the first station we came to. G—— went on, and I saw him no more.

I feared that our applications would be simultaneous, or that we should have an indecorous scuffle for the book in the Land-Office itself. In this case, there would only have remained the unsatisfactory alternative of drawing lots for precedence. There was nothing for it but to go on, and see how matters would turn up. Before midday, and whilst still sixty miles from town, my horse knocked-up completely, and would not go another step. G——'s horse, only two months before, had gone a hundred miles in less than fifteen hours, and was now pitted against mine, which was thoroughly done-up. Rather anticipating this, I had determined on keeping the tracks, thus passing stations where I might have a chance of getting a fresh mount. G—— took a short cut, saving fully ten miles in distance, but travelling over a very stony country, with no track. A track is a great comfort to a horse.

I shall never forget my relief when, at a station where I had already received great kindness, I obtained the loan of a horse that had been taken up that morning from a three-months' spell. No greater service could, at the time, have been rendered me, and I felt that I had indeed met with a friend in need.

The prospect was now brilliant, save that the Rakaia was said to be very heavily freshed. Fearing I might have to swim for it, I left my watch at M——'s, and went on with the satisfactory reflection that, at any rate, if I could not cross, G—— could not do so either. To my delight, however, the river was very low, and I forded it without the smallest difficulty a little before sunset. A few hours afterwards, down it came. I heard that G—— was an hour ahead of me, but this was of no consequence. Riding ten miles farther, and now only twenty-five miles from Christ Church, I called at an accommodation-house, and heard that G—— was within, so went on, and determined to camp and rest my horse. The night was again intensely dark, and it soon came on to rain so heavily that there was nothing for it but to start again for the next accommodation-house, twelve miles from town. I slept there a few hours, and by seven o'clock next morning was in Christ Church. So was G——. We could neither of us do anything till the Land-Office opened at ten o'clock. At twenty minutes before ten I repaired thither, expecting to find G—— in waiting, and anticipating a row. If it came to fists, I should get the worst of it—that was a moral certainty—and I really half-feared something of the kind. To my surprise, the office-doors were open—all the rooms were open—and on reaching that in which the application-book was kept, I found it already upon the table. I opened it with trembling fingers, and saw my adversary's name written in bold handwriting, defying me, as it were, to do my worst.

The clock, as the clerk was ready to witness, was twenty minutes before ten. I learnt from him also that G—— had written his name down about half an hour. This was all right. My course was to wait till after ten, write my name, and oppose G——'s application as having been entered unduly, and before office-hours. I have no doubt that I should have succeeded in gaining my point in this way, but a much easier victory was in store for me.

Running my eye through the list of names, to my great surprise I saw my own among them. It had been entered by my solicitor, on another matter of business, the previous day, but it stood next *below* G——'s. G——'s name, then, had clearly been inserted unfairly, out of due order. The whole thing was made clear to the Commissioners of the Waste Lands, and I need not say that I effected my purchase without difficulty. A few weeks afterwards, allowing him for his hut and yard, I bought G—— out entirely. I will now return to the Rangitata.

There is a large flat on either side of it, sloping very gently down to the river-bed proper, which is from one to two miles across. The one flat belongs to me, and that on the north bank to another. The river is very easily crossed, as it flows in a great many channels; in a fresh, therefore, it is still often fordable. We found it exceedingly low, as the preceding cold had frozen up the sources, whilst the nor'-wester that followed was of short duration, and unaccompanied with the hot tropical rain which causes the freshes. The nor'-westers are vulgarly supposed to cause freshes simply by melting the snow upon the back ranges. We, however, and all who live near the great range, and see the nor'-wester while still among the snowy ranges, know for certain that the river does not rise more than two or three inches, nor lose its beautiful milky blue colour, unless the wind be accompanied with rain upon the great range—rain extending sometimes as low down as the commencement of the plains. These rains are warm and heavy, and make the feed beautifully green.

The nor'-westers are a very remarkable feature in the climate of this settlement. They are excessively violent, sometimes shaking the very house; hot, dry, from having already poured out their moisture, and enervating like the Italian sirocco. The fact seems to be, that the nor'-west winds come heated from the tropics, and charged with moisture from the ocean, and this is precipitated by the ice-fields of the mountains in deluges of rain, chiefly on the western side, but occasionally extending some distance to the east. They blow from two or three hours to as many days, and if they last any length of time, are generally succeeded by a sudden change to sou'-west—the cold, rainy, or snowy wind. We catch the nor'-west in full force, but are sheltered from the sou'-west, which, with us, is a quiet wind, accompanied with gentle drizzling but cold rain, and in the winter, snow.

The nor'-wester is first descried on the river-bed. Through the door of my hut, from which the snowy range is visible, at our early breakfast, I see a lovely summer's morning, breathlessly quiet, and intensely hot. Suddenly a little cloud of dust is driven down the river-bed a mile and a-half off; it increases, till one would think the river was on fire, and that the opposite mountains were obscured by volumes of smoke. Still it is calm with us. By and by, as the day increases, the wind gathers strength, and, extending beyond the river-bed, gives the flats on either side a benefit; then it catches the downs, and generally blows hard till four or five o'clock, when it calms down, and is followed by a cool and tranquil night, delightful to every sense. If, however, the wind does not cease, and it has been raining up the gorges, there will be a fresh; and if the rain has come down any distance from the main range, it will be a heavy fresh; while if there has been a clap or two of thunder (a very rare occurrence), it will be a fresh in which the river will not be fordable. The floods come and go with great rapidity. The river will begin to rise a very few hours after the rain commences, and will generally have subsided to its former level about forty-eight hours after the rain has ceased.

As we generally come in for the tail-end of the nor'-western rains, so we sometimes, though less frequently, get that of the sou'-west winds also. The sou'-west rain comes to us up the river through the lower gorge, and is consequently sou'-east rain with us, owing to the direction of the valley. But it is always called sou'-west if it comes from the southward at all. In fact, there are only three recognised winds, the north-west, the north-east, and the south-west, and I never recollect perceiving the wind to be in any other quarter, saving from local causes. The north-east is most prevalent in summer, and blows with delightful freshness during the greater part of the day, often rendering the hottest weather very pleasant.

It is curious to watch the battle between the north-west and south-east wind, as we often see it. For some days, perhaps, the upper gorges may have been obscured with dark and surging clouds, and the snowy ranges hidden from view. Suddenly the mountains at the lower end of the valley become banked-up with clouds, and the sand begins to blow up the river-bed some miles below, while it is still blowing down with us. The southerly 'burster,' as it is called, gradually creeps up, and at last drives the other off the field. A few chilly puffs, then a great one, and in a minute or two the air becomes cold, even in the height of summer. Indeed, I have seen snow fall on the 12th of January. It was not much, but the air was as cold as in mid-winter.

The force of the south-west wind is here broken by the front ranges, and on these it often leaves its rain or snow, while we are quite exempt from either. We frequently hear both of more rain and of more snow on the plains than we have had, though my hut is at an elevation of 1,840 feet above the level of the sea. On the plains, it will often blow for forty-eight hours, accompanied by torrents of pelting pitiless rain, and is sometimes so violent, that there is hardly any possibility of making headway against it. Sheep race before it as hard as they can go helter-skelter, leaving their lambs behind them to shift for themselves. There is no shelter on the plains, and, unless stopped by the shepherds, they will drive from one river to the next. The shepherds, therefore, have a hard time of it, for they must be out till the wind goes down; and the worse the weather, the more absolutely necessary it is that they should be with the sheep. Different flocks not unfrequently join during these gales, and the nuisance to both the owners is very great.

In the back-country, sheep can always find shelter in the gullies, or under the lee of a mountain.

We have here been singularly favoured with regard to snow this last winter, for whereas I was absolutely detained by the snow upon the plains on my way from Christ Church, because my horse would have had nothing to eat had I gone on, when I arrived at home I found they had been all astonishment as to what could possibly have been keeping me so long away.

The nor'-westers sometimes blow even in mid-winter, but are most frequent in spring and summer, sometimes continuing for a fortnight together.

During a nor'-wester, the sand on the river-bed is blinding, filling eyes, nose, and ears, and stinging sharply every exposed part. I lately had the felicity of getting a small mob of sheep into the river-bed (with a view of crossing them on to my own country) whilst this wind was blowing. There were only between seven and eight hundred, and as we were three, with two dogs, we expected to be able to put them through ourselves. We did so through the two first considerable streams, and then could not get them to move on any farther. As they paused, I will take the opportunity to digress and describe the process of putting sheep across a river.

The first thing is to carefully secure a spot fitted for the purpose, for which the principal requisites are: first, that the current set for the opposite bank, so that the sheep will be carried towards it. Sheep cannot swim against a strong current, and if the stream be flowing evenly down mid-channel, they will be carried down a long way before they land; if, however, it sets at all towards the side from which they started, they will probably be landed by the stream on that same side. Therefore the current should flow towards the opposite bank. Secondly, there must be a good landing-place for the sheep. A spot must not be selected where the current sweeps underneath a hollow bank of gravel or a perpendicular wall of shingle; the bank on to which the sheep are to land must shelve, no matter how steeply, provided it does not rise perpendicularly out of the water. Thirdly, a good place must be chosen for putting them in; the water must not become deep all at once, or the sheep won't face it. It must be shallow at the commencement, so that they may have got too far to recede before they find their mistake. Fourthly, there should be no tutu in the immediate vicinity of either the place where the sheep are put into the river or that on to which they are to come out; for, in spite of your most frantic endeavours, you will be very liable to get some sheep tuted. These requisites being secured, the depth of the water is, of course, a matter of no moment; the narrowness of the stream being a point of far greater importance. These rivers abound in places combining every requisite.

The sheep being mobbed up together near the spot where they are intended to enter the water, the best plan is to split off a small number, say a hundred or hundred and fifty (a larger mob would be less easily managed), dog them, bark at them yourself furiously, beat them, spread out arms and legs to prevent their escaping, and raise all the unpleasant din about their ears that you possibly can. In spite of all that you can do they will very likely break through you and make back; if so, persevere as before, and in about ten minutes a single sheep will be seen eying the opposite bank, and evidently meditating an attempt to gain it. Pause a moment that you interrupt not a consummation so devoutly to be wished; the sheep bounds forward with three or four jumps into mid-stream, is carried down, and thence on to the opposite bank; immediately that one sheep has entered, let one man get into the river below them, and splash water up at them to keep them from working lower and lower down the stream and getting into a bad place; let another be bringing up the remainder of the mob, so that they may have come up before the whole of the leading body are over; if this be done they will cross in a string of their own accord, and there will be no more trouble from the moment when the first sheep entered the water.

If the sheep are obstinate and will not take the water, it is a good plan to haul one or two over first, pulling them through by the near hind leg; these will often entice the others, or a few lambs will encourage their mothers to come over to them, unless indeed they immediately swim back to their mothers: the first was the plan we adopted.

As I said, our sheep were got across the first two streams without much difficulty; then they became completely silly. The awful wind, so high that we could scarcely hear ourselves talk, the blinding sand, the cold glacier water, rendered more chilling by the strong wind, which, contrary to custom, was very cold, all combined to make them quite stupid; the little lambs stuck up their backs and shut their eyes and looked very shaky on their legs, while the bigger ones and the ewes would do nothing but turn round and stare at us. Our dogs, knocked-up completely, and we ourselves were somewhat tired and hungry, partly from night-watching and partly from having fasted since early dawn, whereas it

was now four o'clock. Still we must get the sheep
over somehow, for a heavy fresh was evidently about
to come down; the river was yet low, and could we
get them over before dark they would be at home. I
rode home to fetch assistance and food; these arriving, by our united efforts we got them over every
stream, save the last, before eight o'clock, and then
it became quite dark, and we left them. The wind
changed from very cold to very hot—it literally blew
hot and cold in the same breath. Rain came down
in torrents, six claps of thunder (thunder is very
rare here) followed in succession about midnight,
and very uneasy we all were. Next morning, before
daybreak, we were by the river side; the fresh had
come down, and we crossed over to the sheep with
difficulty, finding them up to their bellies in water
huddled up in a mob together. We shifted them
on to one of the numerous islands, where they were
secure, and had plenty of feed, and with great
difficulty recrossed, the river having greatly risen
since we had got upon its bed. In two days' time
it had gone down sufficiently to allow of our getting
the sheep over, and we did so without the loss of a
single one.

I hardly know why I have introduced this into an
account of a trip with a bullock dray; it is, however, a
colonial incident, such as might happen any day. In a
life of continual excitement one thinks very little of

these things. They may, however, serve to give English readers a glimpse of some of the numerous incidents which, constantly occurring in one shape or other, render the life of a colonist not only endurable, but actually pleasant.

CHAPTER IX.

THE flora of this province is very disappointing, and
the absence of beautiful flowers adds to the uninteresting character which too generally pervades the scenery,
save among the great Southern Alps themselves. There
is no burst of bloom as there is in Switzerland and
Italy, and the trees being, with few insignificant exceptions, all evergreen, the difference between winter and
summer is chiefly perceptible by the state of the grass
and the temperature. I do not know one really pretty
flower which belongs to the plains; I believe there are
one or two, but they are rare, and form no feature in
the landscape. I never yet saw a blue flower growing
wild here, nor indeed one of any other colour but
white or yellow; if there are such they do not prevail,
and their absence is sensibly felt. We have no solda-
nellas and auriculas, and alpine cowslips, no brilliant
gentians and anemones. We have one very stupid white
gentian; but it is, to say the least of it, uninteresting

to a casual observer. We have violets, very like those
at home, but they are small and white, and have no
scent. We have also a daisy, very like the English, but
not nearly so pretty; we have a great ugly sort of
Michaelmas Daisy too, and any amount of Spaniard.
I do not say but that by hunting on the peninsula,
one might find one or two beautiful species, but
simply that on the whole the flowers are few and ugly.
The only plant good to eat is Maori cabbage, and that
is Swede turnip gone wild, from seed left by Captain
Cook. Some say it is indigenous, but I do not believe
it. The Maoris carry the seed about with them, and
sow it wherever they camp. I should rather write,
used to sow it where they *camped*, for the Maoris in
this island are almost a thing of the past.

The root of the Spaniard, it should be added, will
support life for some little time.

Tutu (pronounced toot) is a plant which abounds
upon the plains for some few miles near the river-beds ;
it is at first sight not much unlike myrtle, but is in
reality a wholly different sort of plant; it dies down in
the winter, and springs up again from its old roots.
These roots are sometimes used for firewood, and are
very tough, so much so as not unfrequently to break
ploughs. It is poisonous for sheep and cattle if eaten
on an empty stomach.

New Zealand is rich in ferns. We have a tree-fern
which grows as high as twenty feet. We have also

some of the English species; among them I believe
the Hymenophyllum tunbridgense, with many of
the same tribe. I see a little fern which, to my eyes,
is our English Asplenium Trichomanes. Every English fern which I know has a variety something like
it here, though seldom identical. We have one to cor-
respond with the adder's tongue and moonwort, with the
Adiantum nigrum and Capillus Veneris, with the Blech-
num boreale, with the Ceterach and Ruta muraria, and
with the Cystopterids. I never saw a Woodsia here;
but I think that every other English family is represented, and that we have many more besides. On the
whole, the British character of many of the ferns is
rather striking, as indeed is the case with our birds and
insects; but, with a few conspicuous exceptions, the
old country has greatly the advantage over us.

The cabbage-tree or ti palm is not a true palm,
though it looks like one. It has not the least resemblance to a cabbage. It has a tuft of green leaves,
which are rather palmy looking at a distance, and
which springs from the top of a pithy, worthless stem,
varying from one to twenty or thirty feet in height.
Sometimes the stem is branched at the top, and each
branch ends in a tuft. The flax and the cabbage-tree
and the tussock-grass are the great botanical features of
the country. Add fern and tutu, and for the back
country, spear-grass and Irishman, and we have summed
up such prevalent plants as strike the eye.

As for the birds, they appear at first sight very few indeed. On the plains one sees a little lark with two white feathers in the tail, and in other respects exactly like the English skylark, save that he does not soar, and has only a little chirrup instead of song. There are also paradise ducks, hawks, terns, red-bills, and sand-pipers, seagulls, and occasionally, though very rarely, a quail.

The paradise duck is a very beautiful bird. The male appears black, with white on the wing, when flying: when on the ground, however, he shows some dark greys and glossy greens and russets, which make him very handsome. He is truly a goose, and not a duck. He says 'whiz' through his throat, and dwells a long time upon the 'z.' He is about the size of a farm-yard duck. The plumage of the female is really gorgeous. Her head is pure white, and her body beautifully coloured with greens and russets and white. She screams, and does not say 'whiz.' Her mate is much fonder of her than she is of him, for if *she* is wounded, he will come to see what is the matter, whereas if *he* is hurt, his base partner flies instantly off and seeks new wedlock, affording a fresh example of the superior fidelity of the male to the female sex. When they have young, they feign lameness, like the plover. I have several times been thus tricked by them. One soon, however, becomes an old bird oneself, and is not to be caught with such chaff any more.

We look about for the young ones, clip off the top
joint·of one wing, and leave them; thus, in a few
months time, we can get prime young ducks for the
running after them. The old birds are very bad eating.
I rather believe they are aware of this, for they are
very bold, and come very close to us. There are two that
constantly come within ten yards of my hut, and I hope
mean to build in the neighbourhood, for the eggs are
excellent. Being geese, and not ducks, they eat grass.
The young birds are called flappers till they can fly,
and can be run down easily.

The hawk is simply a large hawk, and to the unscientific nothing more. There is a small sparrow
hawk too, which is very bold, and which will attack a
man if he goes near its nest.

The tern is a beautiful little bird about twice as
big as a swallow, and somewhat resembling it in its
flight, but much more graceful. It has a black satin
head, and lavender satin and white over the rest of its
body. It has an orange bill and feet; and is not seen
in the back country during the winter.

The red-bill is, I believe, identical with the oyster-
catcher of the Cornish coast. It has a long orange bill,
and orange feet, and is black and white over the body.

The sand-piper is very like the lark in plumage.

The quail is nearly exterminated. It is exactly like
a small partridge, and is most excellent eating. Ten
years ago it was very abundant, but now it is very

rarely seen. The poor little thing is entirely defence-
less; it cannot take more than three flights, and then it
is done up. Some say the fires have destroyed them;
some say the sheep have trod on their eggs; some that
they have all been hunted down: my own opinion is that
the wild cats, which have increased so as to be very
numerous, have driven the little creatures nearly off
the face of the earth.

There are wood hens also on the plains; but, though
very abundant, they are not much seen. The wood hen
is a bird rather resembling the pheasant tribe in plumage, but not so handsome. It has a long sharp bill
and long feet. It is about the size of a hen. It cannot fly, but sticks its little bob-tail up and down whenever it walks, and has a curious Paul-Pry-like gait,
which is rather amusing. It is exceedingly bold, and
will come sometimes right into a house. It is an arrant
thief, moreover, and will steal anything. I know of a
case in which one was seen to take up a gold watch,
and run off with it, and of another in which a number
of men, who were camping out, left their pannikins at
the camp, and on their return found them all gone, and
only recovered them by hearing the wood hens tapping
their bills against them. Anything bright excites their
greed; anything red, their indignation. They are
reckoned good eating by some; but most people think
them exceedingly rank and unpleasant. From fat wood
hens a good deal of oil can be got, and this oil is very

valuable for almost anything where oil is wanted.   It is sovereign for rheumatics, and wounds or bruises; item for softening one's boots, and so forth.   The egg is about the size of a guinea fowl's, dirtily streaked, and spotted with a dusky purple; it is one of the best eating eggs I have ever tasted.

I must not omit to mention the white crane, a very beautiful bird, with immense wings, of the purest white; and the swamp hen, with a tail which it is constantly bobbing up and down like the wood hen; it has a good deal of bluish purple about it, and is very handsome.

There are other birds on the plains, especially about the river-beds, but not many worthy of notice.

In the back country, however, we have a considerable variety.   I have mentioned the kaka and the parroquet.

The robin is a pretty little fellow, in build and manners very like our English robin, but tamer.   His plumage, however, is different, for he has a dusky black tail coat and a pale canary-coloured waistcoat.   When one is camping out, no sooner has one lit one's fire than several robins make their appearance, prying into one's whole proceedings with true robin-like impudence. They have never probably seen a fire before, and are rather puzzled by it.   I heard of one which first lighted on the embers, which were covered with ashes; finding this unpleasant, he hopped on to a burning twig; this was worse, so the third time he lighted on a red-hot coal; whereat, much disgusted, he took himself off, I hope escaping with nothing but a blistered toe. They frequently come into my hut. I watched one hop in a few mornings ago, when the breakfast things were set. First he tried the bread—that was good; then he tried the sugar—that was good also ; then he tried the salt, which he instantly rejected ; and, lastly, he tried a cup of hot tea, on which he flew away. I have seen them light on a candle (not a lighted one) and peck the tallow. I fear, however, that these tame ones are too often killed by the cats.

The tomtit is like its English namesake in shape, but smaller, and with a glossy black head and bright yellow breast.

The wren is a beautiful little bird, much smaller than the English one, and with green about its plumage.

The tui or parson-bird is a starling, and has a small tuft of white cravat-like feathers growing from his throat. True to his starling nature, he has a delicious voice.

We have a thrush, but it is rather rare. It is just like the English, save that it has some red feathers in his tail.

Our teal is, if not the same as the English teal, so like it, that the difference is not noticeable.

Our linnet is a little larger than the English, with a clear bell-like voice, as of a blacksmith's hammer on an anvil. Indeed, we might call him the harmonious blacksmith.

The pigeon is larger than the English, and far handsomer. He has much white and glossy green shot with
purple about him, and is one of the most beautiful birds I
ever saw. He is very foolish, and can be noosed with ease.
Tie a string with a noose at the end of it to a long stick,
and you may put it round his neck and catch him. The
kakas too will let you do this, and in a few days become
quite tame.

Besides these, there is an owl or two. These are
heard occasionally, but not seen. Often at night one
hears a solemn cry of 'More pork! more pork! more
pork!' I have heard people talk too of a laughing
jackass (not the Australian bird of that name), but no
one has ever seen it.

Occasionally we hear rumours of the footprint of a
moa, and the Nelson surveyors found fresh foot-tracks
of a bird, which were measured for fourteen inches. Of
this there can be little doubt; but since a wood hen's foot
measures four inches, and a wood hen does not stand
higher than a hen, fourteen inches is hardly long enough
for the track of a moa, the largest kind of which stood
fifteen feet high. We often find some of their bones
lying in a heap upon the ground, but never a perfect
skeleton. Little heaps of their gizzard stones too are
constantly found. They consist of very smooth and
polished flints and cornelians, with sometimes quartz.
The bird generally chose rather pretty stones. I do
not remember finding a single sandstone specimen of a

moa gizzard stone. These heaps are easily distinguished, and very common. Few people believe in the existence of a moa. If one or two be yet living, they will probably be found on the west coast, that yet unexplored region of forest which may contain sleeping princesses and gold in ton blocks, and all sorts of good things. A gentleman who lives at the Kaikoras possesses a moa's egg; it is ten inches by seven. It was discovered in a Maori grave, and must have been considered precious at the time it was buried, for the Maoris were accustomed to bury a man's valuables with him.

I really know of few other birds to tell you about. There is a good sprinkling more, but they form no feature in the country, and are only interesting to the naturalist. There is the kiwi, or apteryx, which is about as large as a turkey, but only found on the west coast. There is a green ground parrot too, called the kakapo, a night bird, and hardly ever found on the eastern side of the island. There is also a very rare, and as yet unnamed kind of kaka, much larger and handsomer than the kaka itself, of which I and another shot one of the first, if not the very first, observed specimen. Being hungry, far from home, and without meat, we ate the interesting creature, but made a note of it for the benefit of science. Since then it has found its way into more worthy hands, and was, a few months ago, sent home to be named. Altogether, I am acquainted with about seventy species of birds belonging to the

Canterbury settlement, and I do not think that there are many more. Two albatrosses came to my wool-shed about seven months ago, and a dead one was found at Mount Peel not long since. I did not see the former myself, but my cook, who was a sailor, watched them for some time, and his word may be taken. I believe, however, that their coming so far inland is a very rare occurrence here.

As for the quadrupeds of New Zealand, they are easily disposed of. There are but two, a kind of rat, which is now banished by the Norway rat, and an animal of either the otter or beaver species, which is known rather by rumour than by actual certainty.

The fishes too will give us little trouble. There are only a sort of minnow and an eel. This last grows to a great size, and is abundant even in the clear rapid, snow-fed rivers. In every creek one may catch eels, and they are excellent eating, if they be cooked in such a manner as to get rid of the oil.

> Try them spitchcocked or stewed,
> They're too oily when fried,

as Barham says, with his usual good sense. I am told that, the other night, a great noise was heard in the kitchen of a gentleman with whom I have the honour to be acquainted, and that the servants, getting up, found an eel chasing a cat round about the room. I believe this story. The eel was in a bucket of water, and doomed to die upon the morrow. Doubtless the

cat had attempted to take liberties with him; on which
a sudden thought struck the eel that he might as well
eat the cat as the cat eat him; and he was preparing to
suit the action to the word, when he was discovered.

The insects are insignificant and ugly, and, like the
plants, devoid of general interest. There is one rather
pretty butterfly, like our English tortoiseshell. There
is a sprinkling of beetles, a few ants, and a detestable.
sandfly, that, on quiet cloudy mornings, especially near
water, is more irritating than can be described. This
little beast is rather venomous; and, for the first fortnight or so that I was bitten by it, every bite swelled
up to a little hard button. Soon, however, one becomes
casehardened, and only suffers the immediate annoyance
consequent upon its tickling and pricking. There is
also a large assortment of spiders. We have, too, one
of the ugliest-looking creatures that I have ever seen.
It is called 'weta,' and is of tawny scorpion-like colour,
with long antennæ and great eyes, and nasty squashy-
looking body, with (I think) six legs. It is a kind of
animal which no one would wish to touch : if touched,
it will bite sharply, some say venomously. It is very
common, but not often seen, and lives chiefly among
dead wood and under stones. In the North Island, I
am told that it grows to the length of three or four
inches. Here I never saw it longer than an inch and
a half. The principal reptile is an almost ubiquitous
lizard.

Summing up, then, the whole of the vegetable and animal productions of this settlement, I think that it is not too much to say that they are decidedly inferior in beauty and interest to those of the old world. You will think that I have a prejudice against the natural history of Canterbury. I assure you I have no such thing; and I believe that any one, on arriving here, would receive a similar impression with myself.

CHAPTER X.

IN looking for a run, some distance must be traversed; the country near Christchurch is already stocked. The waste lands are, indeed, said to be wholly taken up throughout the colony, wherever they are capable of supporting sheep. It may, however, be a matter of some satisfaction to a new settler to examine this point for himself, and to consider what he requires in the probable event of having to purchase the good-will of a run, with the improvements upon it, which can hardly be obtained under 150*l.* per 1,000 acres.

A river boundary is most desirable; the point above or below the confluence of two rivers is still better, as there are then only two sides to guard. Stony ground must not be considered as an impediment; grass grows between the stones, and a dray can travel upon it. England must have been a most impracticable country to traverse before metalled roads were made. Here the surface is almost everywhere a compact mass of shingle;

it is for the most part only near the sea that the shingle
is covered with soil.   Forest and swamp are much
greater impediments to a journey than a far greater
distance of hard ground would prove.   A river such as
the Cam or Ouse would be far more difficult to cross
without bridges than the Rakaia or Rangitata, notwith-
standing their volume and rapidity; the former are
deep in mud, and rarely have convenient places at which
to get in or out; while the latter abound in them, and
have a stony bed on which the wheels of your dray
make no impression.   The stony ground will carry a
sheep to each acre and a half or two acres.   Such
diseases as foot-rot are unknown, owing probably to the
generally dry surface of the land.

There are few Maoris here; they inhabit the north
island, and are only in small numbers, and degenerate
in this, so may be passed over unnoticed.   The only
effectual policy in dealing with them is to show a bold
front, and, at the same time, do them a good turn whenever you can be quite certain that your kindness will
not be misunderstood as a symptom of fear.   There are
no wild animals that will molest your sheep.   In
Australia they have to watch the flocks night and day
because of the wild dogs.   The yards, of course, are not
proof against dogs, and the Australian shepherd's hut
is built close against the yard; here this is unnecessary.

Having settled that you will take up your country or
purchase the lease of it, you must consider next how to

get a dray on to it. Horses are not to be thought of except for riding; you must buy a dray and bullocks. The rivers here are not navigable.

Wages are high. People do not leave England and go to live at the antipodes to work for the same wages which they had at home. They want to better themselves as well as you do, and the supply being limited, they will ask and get from 1*l.* to 30*s.* a week besides their board and billet.

You must remember you will have a rough life at first; there will be a good deal of cold and exposure; a good deal of tent work; possibly a fever or two; to say nothing of the seeds of rheumatism which will give you something to meditate upon hereafter.

You and your men will have to be on rather a different footing from that on which you stood in England. There, if your servant were in any respect what you did not wish, you were certain of getting plenty of others to take his place. Here, if a man does not find you quite what he wishes, he is certain of getting plenty of others to employ him. In fact, he is at a premium, and soon finds this out. On really good men this produces no other effect than a demand for high wages. They will be respectful and civil, though there will be a slight but quite unobjectionable difference in their manner toward you. Bad men assume an air of defiance which renders their immediate dismissal a matter of necessity. When you have good men, however, you

must recognise the different position in which you
stand toward them as compared with that which sub-
sisted at home.   The fact is, they are more your equals
and more independent of you, and, this being the case,
you must treat them accordingly.   I do not advise you
for one moment to submit to disrespect ; this would be
a fatal error.   A man whose conduct does not satisfy
you must be sent about his business as certainly as in
England; but when you have men who *do* suit you,
you must, besides paying them handsomely, expect them
to treat you rather as an English yeoman would speak
to the squire of his parish than as an English labourer
would speak to him.   The labour markets will not be so
bad but that good men can be had, and as long as you
put up with bad men it serves you right to be the loser
by your weakness.

Some good hands are very improvident, and will for
the most part spend their money in drinking, a very
short time after they have earned it.   They will come
back possibly with a *dead horse to work off*—that is, a
debt at the accommodation house—and will work hard
for another year to have another drinking bout at the
end of it.   This is a thing fatally common here.   Such
men are often first-rate hands and thoroughly good
fellows when away from drink ; but, on the whole,
saving men are perhaps the best.   Commend yourself
to a good screw for a shepherd ; if he knows the value
of money he knows the value of lambs, and if he has

contracted the habit of being careful with his own money he will be apt to be so with yours also. But in justice to the improvident, it must be owned they are often admirable men save in the one point of sobriety.

Their political knowledge is absolutely nil, and, were the colony to give them political power, it might as well give gunpowder to children.

How many hands shall you want?

We will say a couple of good bush hands, who will put up your hut and yards and wool-shed. If you are in a hurry and have plenty of money you can have more. Besides these you will want a bullock driver and shepherd, unless you are shepherd yourself. You must manage the cooking among you as best you can, and must be content to wash up yourself, taking your full part in the culinary processes, or you will soon find disaffection in the camp; but if you can afford to have a cook, have one by all means. It is a great nuisance to come in from a long round after sheep and find the fire out and no hot water to make tea, and to have to set to work immediately to get your men's supper; for they cannot earn their supper and cook it at the same time. The difficulty is that good boys are hard to get, and a man that is worth anything at all will hardly take to cooking as a profession. Hence it comes to pass that the cooks are generally indolent and dirty fellows, who don't like hard work. Your college education, if you have had one, will doubtless have made you familiar with the art

of making bread; you will now proceed to discover the
mysteries of boiling potatoes. The uses of dripping
will begin to dawn upon you, and you will soon become
expert in the manufacture of tallow candles. You will
wash your own clothes, and will learn that you must
not boil flannel shirts, and experience will teach you
that you must eschew the promiscuous use of washing
soda, tempting though indeed it be if you are in a
hurry. If you use collars, I can inform you that Glen-
field starch is the only starch used in the laundries of
our most gracious Sovereign; I tell you this in confidence, as it is not generally advertised.

To return to the culinary department. Your natural
poetry of palate will teach you the proper treatment of
the onion, and you will ere long be able to handle that
inestimable vegetable with the breadth yet delicacy
which it requires. Many other things you will learn,
which for your sake as well as my own I will not enume-
rate here. Let the above suffice for examples.

At first your wethers will run with your ewes, and
you will only want one shepherd; but as soon as the
mob gets up to two or three thousand the wethers
should be kept separate; you will then want another
shepherd. As soon as you have secured your run you
must buy sheep; otherwise you lose time, as the run is
only valuable for the sheep it carries. Bring sheep,
shepherd, men, stores, all at one and the same time.
Some wethers must be included in your purchase,

otherwise you will run short of meat, as none of your own breeding will be ready for the knife for a year and a half, to say the least of it. No wether should be killed till it is two years old, and then it is murder to kill an animal which brings you in such good interest by its wool, and would even be better if suffered to live three years longer, when you will have had its value in its successive fleeces. It will, however, pay you better to invest nearly all your money in ewes, and to kill your own young stock, than to sink more capital than is absolutely necessary in wethers.

Start your dray, then, from town and join it with your sheep on the way up. Your sheep will not travel more than ten miles a day if you are to do them justice; so your dray must keep pace with them. You will generally find plenty of firewood on the track. You can camp under the dray at night. In about a week you will get on to your run, and very glad you will feel when you are safely come to the end of your journey. See the horses properly looked to at once; then set up the tent, make a good fire, put the kettle on, out with the frying-pan and get your supper, smoke the calumet of peace, and go to bed.

The first question is, Where shall you place your homestead? You must put it in such a situation as will be most convenient for working the sheep. These are the real masters of the place—the run is theirs, not yours : you cannot bear this in mind too diligently.

All considerations of pleasantness of site must succumb to this. You must fix on such a situation as not to cut up the run, by splitting off a little corner too small to give the sheep free scope and room. They will fight rather shy of your homestead, you may be certain; so the homestead must be out of their way. You *must*, however, have water and firewood at hand, which is a great convenience, to say nothing of the saving of labour and expense. Therefore, if you can find a bush near a stream, make your homestead on the lee side of it. A stream is a boundary, and your hut, if built in such a position, will interfere with your sheep as little as possible.

The sheep will make for rising ground and hill-side to camp at night, and generally feed with their heads up the wind, if it is not too violent. As your mob increases, you can put an out-station on the other side the run.

In order to prevent the sheep straying beyond your boundaries, keep ever hovering at a distance round them, so far off that they shall not be disturbed by your presence, and even be ignorant that you are looking at them. Sheep cannot be too closely watched, or too much left to themselves. You must remember they are your masters, and not you theirs; you exist for them, not they for you. If you bear this well in mind, you will be able to turn the tables on them effectually at shearing-time. But if you once begin to make the sheep suit their feeding-hours to your convenience, you may as well give up sheep-farming at once. You will soon find the mob begin to look poor, your percentage of lambs will fall off, and in fact you will have to pay very heavily for saving your own trouble, as indeed would be the case in every occupation or profession you might adopt.

Of course you will have to turn your sheep back when they approach the boundary of your neighbour. Be ready, then, at the boundary. You have been watching them creeping up in a large semicircle toward the forbidden ground. As long as they are on their own run let them alone, give them not a moment's anxiety of mind; but directly they reach the boundary, show yourself with your dog in your most terrific aspect. Startle them, frighten them, disturb their peace; do so again and again, at the same spot, from the very first day. Let them always have peace on their own run, and none anywhere off it. In a month or two you will find the sheep begin to understand your meaning, and it will then be very easy work to keep them within bounds. If, however, you suffer them to have half an hour now and then on the forbidden territory, they will be constantly making for it. The chances are that the feed is good on or about the boundary, and they will be seduced by this to cross, and go on and on till they are quite beyond your control.

You will have burnt a large patch of feed on the outset.

Burn it in early spring, on a day when rain appears to be at hand. It is dangerous to burn too much at once: a large fire may run farther than you wish, and, being no respecter of imaginary boundaries, will cross on to your neighbour's run without compunction and without regard to his sheep, and then heavy damages will be brought against you. Burn, however, you must; so do it carefully. Light one strip first, and keep putting it out by beating it with leafy branches. This will form a fireproof boundary between you and your neighbour.

Burnt feed means contented and well-conditioned sheep. The delicately-green and juicy grass which springs up after burning is far better for sheep than the rank and dry growth of summer after it has been withered by the winter's frosts. Your sheep will not ramble, for if they have plenty of burnt pasture they are contented where they are. They feed in the morning, bunch themselves together in clusters during the heat of the day, and feed again at night.

Moreover, on burnt pasture, no fire can come down upon you from your neighbour so as to hurt your sheep.

The day will come when you will have no more occasion for burning, when your run will be fully stocked, and the sheep will keep your feed so closely cropped that it will do without it. It is certainly a mortification to see volumes of smoke rising into the air, and to know that all that smoke might have been wool, and might have been sold by you for 2s. a pound in England. You will think it great waste, and regret that you have not more sheep to eat it. However, that will come to pass in time; and meanwhile, if you have not mouths enough upon your run to make wool of it, you must burn it off and make smoke of it instead. There is sure to be a good deal of rough scrub and brushwood on the run, which is better destroyed, and which sheep would not touch; therefore, for the ultimate value of your run, it is as well or better that it should be fired than fed off.

The very first work to be done after your arrival will be to make a yard. for your sheep. Make this large enough to hold five or six times as many sheep as you possess at first. It may be square in shape. Place two good large gates at the middle of either of the two opposite sides. This will be sufficient at first, but, as your flocks increase, a somewhat more complicated arrangement will be desirable.

The sheep, we will suppose, are to be thoroughly overhauled. You wish, for some reason, to inspect their case fully yourself, or you must tail your lambs, in which case every lamb has to be caught, and you will cut its tail off, and ear-mark it with your own ear-mark; or, again, you will see fit to draft out all the lambs that are ready for weaning; or you may wish to cull the mob, and sell off the worst-woolled sheep; or your neighbour's sheep may have joined with yours; or for many other reasons it is necessary that your flock should be closely examined. Without good yards it is impossible to do this well—they are an essential of the highest importance.

Select, then, a site as dry and stony as possible (for your sheep will have to be put into the yard over night), and at daylight in the morning set to work.

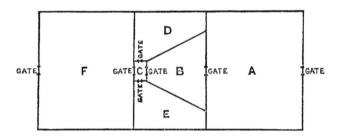

Fill the yard B with sheep from the big yard A. The yard B we will suppose to hold about 600. Fill C from B : C shall hold about 100. When the sheep are in that small yard C (which is called the drafting-yard), you can overhaul them, and your men can catch the lambs and hold them up to you over the rail of the yard to ear-mark and tail. There being but 100 sheep in the yard, you can easily run your eye over them. Should you be drafting out sheep or taking your rams out, let the sheep which you are taking out be let into the yards D and E. Or, it may be, you are drafting two different sorts of sheep at once; then there will be two

yards in which to put them. When you have done with
the small mob, let it out into the yard F, taking the
tally of the sheep as they pass through the gate. This
gate, therefore, must be a small one, so as not to admit
more than one or two at a time. It would be tedious
work filling the small yard c from the big one A; for
in that large space the sheep will run about, and it will
take you some few minutes every time. From the
smaller yard B, however, c will easily be filled. Among
the other great advantages of good yards, there is none
greater than the time saved. This is of the highest importance, for the ewes will be hungry, and their lambs
will have sucked them dry ; and then, as soon as they are
turned out of the yards, the mothers will race off after
feed, and the lambs, being weak, will lag behind ; and
the Merino ewe being a bad mother, the two may never
meet again, and the lamb will die. Therefore it is
essential to begin work of this sort early in the morning, and to have yards so constructed as to cause as little
loss of time as possible. I will not say that the plan
given above is the very best that could be devised,
but it is common out here, and answers all practical
purposes. The weakest point is in the approach to
B from A.

As soon as you have done with the mob, let them out.
They will race off helter-skelter to feed, and soon be
spread out in an ever-widening fan-like shape. Therefore have some one stationed a good way off to check

their first burst, and stay them from going too far and leaving their lambs; after a while, as you sit, telescope in hand, you will see the ewes come bleating back to the yards for their lambs. They have satisfied the first cravings of their hunger, and their motherly feelings are beginning to return. Now, if the sheep have not been kept a little together, the lambs may have gone off after the ewes, and some few will then be pretty certain never to find their mothers again. It is rather a pretty sight to sit on a bank and watch the ewes coming back. There is sure to be a mob of a good many lambs sticking near the yards, and ewe after ewe will come back and rush up affectionately to one lamb after another. A good few will try to palm themselves off upon her. If she is young and foolish, she will be for a short time in doubt; if she is older and wiser, she will butt away the little impostors with her head; but they are very importunate, and will stick to her for a long while. At last, however, she finds her true child, and is comforted. She kisses its nose and tail with the most affectionate fondness, and soon the lost lamb is seen helping himself lustily, and frolicking with his tail in the height of his contentment. I have known, however, many cunning lambs make a practice of thieving from the more inexperienced ewes, though they have mothers of their own; and I remember one very beautiful and favourite lamb of mine, who, to my great sorrow, lost its mother, but kept itself alive in this manner, and throve and grew up to be a splendid sheep by mere roguery. Such a case is an exception, not a rule.

You may perhaps wonder how you are to know that your sheep are all right, and that none get away. You cannot be *quite certain* of this. You may be pretty sure, however, for you will soon have a large number of sheep with whom you are personally acquainted, and who have, from time to time, forced themselves upon your attention either by peculiar beauty or peculiar ugliness, or by having certain marks upon them. You will have a black sheep or two, and probably a long-tailed one or two, and a sheep with only one eye, and another with a wart on its nose, and so forth. These will be your marked sheep, and if you find all of them you may be satisfied that the rest are safe also. Your eye will soon become very accurate in telling you the number of a mob of sheep.

When the sheep are lambing, they should not be disturbed. You cannot meddle with a mob of lambing ewes without doing them mischief. Some one or two lambs, or perhaps many more, will be lost every time you disturb the flock. The young sheep, until they have had their lambs a few days, and learnt their value, will leave them upon the slightest provocation. Then there is a serious moral injury inflicted upon the ewe: she becomes familiar with the crime of infanticide, and will be apt to leave her next lamb as carelessly as her first. If, however, she has once reared a lamb, she will be fond of the next, and, when old, will face anything, even a dog, for the sake of her child.

When, therefore, the sheep are lambing, you must ride or walk farther round, and notice any tracks you may see : anything rather than disturb the sheep. They must always lamb on burnt or green feed, and against the best boundary you have, and then there will be the less occasion to touch them.

Besides the yards above described, you will want one or two smaller ones for getting the sheep into the wool-shed at shearing-time, and you will also want a small yard for branding. The wool-shed is a roomy covered building, with a large central space, and an aisle-like partition on each side. These last will be for holding the sheep during the night. The shearers will want to begin with daylight, and the dew will not yet be off the wool if the sheep are exposed. If wool is packed damp it will heat and spoil; therefore a sufficient number of sheep must be left under cover through the night to last the shearers till the dew is off. In a wool-shed the aisles would be called skilions (whence the name is derived I know not, nor whether it has two *l*'s in it or one). All the sheep go into the skilions. The shearers shear in the centre, which is large enough to leave room for the wool to be stowed away at one end. The shearers pull the sheep out of the skilions as they want them. Each picks the worst sheep, i. e. that with the least wool upon it, that happens to be at hand at the time, trying to put the best-wooled sheep, which are consequently the hardest to shear, upon some one else; and so the heaviest-wooled and largest sheep get shorn the last.

A good man will shear 100 sheep in a day, some even more; but 100 is reckoned good work. I have known 195 sheep to be shorn by one man in a day; but I fancy these must have been from an old and bare mob, and that this number of well-wooled sheep would be quite beyond one man's power. Sheep are not shorn so neatly as at home. But supposing a man has a mob of 20,000, he must get the wool off their backs as best he can without carping at an occasional snip from a sheep's carcass. If the wool is taken close off, and only now and then a sheep snipped, there will be no cause to complain.

Then follows the draying of the wool to port, and the bullocks come in for their full share of work. It is a pleasant sight to see the first load of wool start down, but a far pleasanter to see the dray returning from its last trip.

Shearing well over will be a weight off your mind. This is your most especially busy and anxious time of year, and when the wool is safely down you will be glad indeed.

It may have been a matter of question with you, Shall I wash my sheep before shearing or not? If you wash them at all, you should do it thoroughly, and take considerable pains to have them clean ; otherwise you had better shear in the grease, i. e. not wash. Wool in the grease weighs about one-third heavier, and consequently fetches a lower price in the market. When wool falls, moreover, the fall tells first upon greasy wool. Still many shear in the grease, and some consider it pays them better to do so. It is a mooted point, but the general opinion is in favour of washing.

As soon as you have put up one yard, you may set to work upon a hut for yourself and men. This you will make of split wooden slabs set upright in the ground, and nailed on to a wall-plate. You will first plant large posts at each of the corners, and one at either side every door, and four for the chimney. At the top of these you will set your wall-plates ; to the wall-plates you will nail your slabs ; on the inside of the slabs you will nail light rods of wood, and plaster them over with mud, having first, however, put up the roof and thatched it. Three or four men will have split the stuff and put up the hut in a fortnight. We will suppose it to be about 18 feet by 12.

By and by, as you grow richer, you may burn bricks at your leisure, and eventually build a brick house. At first, however, you must rough it.

You will set about a garden at once. You will bring up fowls at once. Pigs may wait till you have time to put up a regular stye, and to have grown potatoes enough to feed them. Two fat and well-tended pigs are worth half a dozen half-starved wretches. Such neglected brutes make a place look very untidy, and their existence will be a burden to themselves, and an eyesore to you.

In a year or two you will find yourself very comfortable. You will get a little fruit from your garden in summer, and will have a prospect of much more. You will have cows, and plenty of butter and milk and eggs ; you will have pigs, and, if you choose it, bees, plenty of vegetables, and, in fact, may live upon the fat of the land, with very little trouble, and almost as little expense. If you grudge this, your fare will be rather unvaried, and will consist solely of tea, mutton, bread, and possibly potatoes. For the first year, these are all you must expect; the second will improve matters ; and the third should see you surrounded with luxuries.

If you are your own shepherd, which at first is more than probable, you will find that shepherding is one of the most prosaic professions you could have adopted. Sheep will be the one idea in your mind ; and as for poetry, nothing will be farther from your thoughts. Your eye will ever be straining after a distant sheep— your ears listening for a bleat—in fact, your whole attention will be directed, the whole day long, to nothing but your flock. Were you to shepherd too long your wits would certainly go wool-gathering, even if you were not tempted to bleat. It is, however, a gloriously-healthy employment.

M

And now, gentle reader, I wish you luck with your run. If you have tolerably good fortune, in a very short time you will be a rich man. Hoping that this may be the case, there remains nothing for me but to wish you heartily farewell.

LONDON

PRINTED BY SPOTTISWOODE AND CO.

NEW-STREET SQUARE